THE LITTLE BIG BOOK OF DISNEY

hello folks!

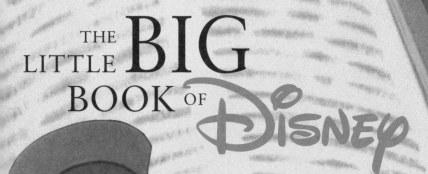

THE LITTLE BIG BOOK OF DISNEY

Text by **Monique Peterson**
Design by **Jon Glick**

A WELCOME BOOK

DISNEY EDITIONS

NEW YORK

PHOTOGRAPHY CREDITS:
Photos on pp. 2 and 142 used by the kind permission
of Mr. Buddy Ebsen; pp. 28, 320–321, used by the
gracious courtesy of Mrs. Virginia Davis McGhee;
pp. 64–65, courtesy of Lucille Ryman-Carroll; p. 65,
from the collection of Nanette Latchford; p. 118 by
John Gilman; p. 145, by Zac Zimmerman; pp.
164–165 by Joan Marcus; p. 207, by Jerry Lee; p. 238
by Topher Dune.

For information address:
Disney Editions
114 Fifth Avenue
New York, New York 10011

Editorial Director: Wendy Lefkon
Senior Editor: Sara Baysinger
Assistant Editor: Jody Revenson

Produced by:
Welcome Enterprises, Inc.
588 Broadway
New York, New York 10012

Project Director: Alice Wong
Designer: Jon Glick

Library of Congress Cataloging-in-Publication Data
on file.

Printed in Singapore by Tien Wah Press
First Edition
10 9 8 7 6 5 4 3 2 1

CONTENTS

ON THE AIR

MAGIC KINGDOMS

WHAT CHARACTERS!

SHEET 2

MUSIC & MELODIES

STORIES & HISTORIES

S EEN FROM A DISTANCE, the Walt Disney Company, like many very large businesses, appears almost monolithic. But step a little closer, and its smaller parts begin to stand out in sharper relief. And, needless to say, the closer one comes, the more the smaller parts begin to stand out, until the broader vision very nearly disappears and all that's left are the details.

That's what this "Little Big Book" is all about—all the wonderful details, the little-known facts that make up the wondrous and multifaceted world of the Disney organization. I think reading this book is a little like having an infinitely variable zoom lens, capable of peering into all the nooks and crannies, both past and present, that make up the world of Disney.

Our history, if you choose Walt Disney's birth as your starting point, is now one hundred years long, and incredibly rich in detail. Many of those details have long since faded into obscurit, if not downright oblivion. It's our hope that this book will serve as a gentle and entertaining reminder that, no matter how the company has grown, it's the people who create the details that have always mattered the most.

FOREWORD
BY ROY E. DISNEY

I hope it will also remind the reader of the broadness of our history— from the barnyard animals in Marceline, Missouri that inspired the creation of Mickey and his pals—to the amazing string of technological inventions that continue to this day, and from the *True-Life Adventures* to Disney's Animal Kingdom; from Anaheim and Orlando to Tokyo, Paris, and Hong Kong; from "When You Wish Upon a Star" to "You'll Be in My Heart."

Most of all, I hope it will stir the same warm memories in you that it does in me, and in all of those who helped create it.

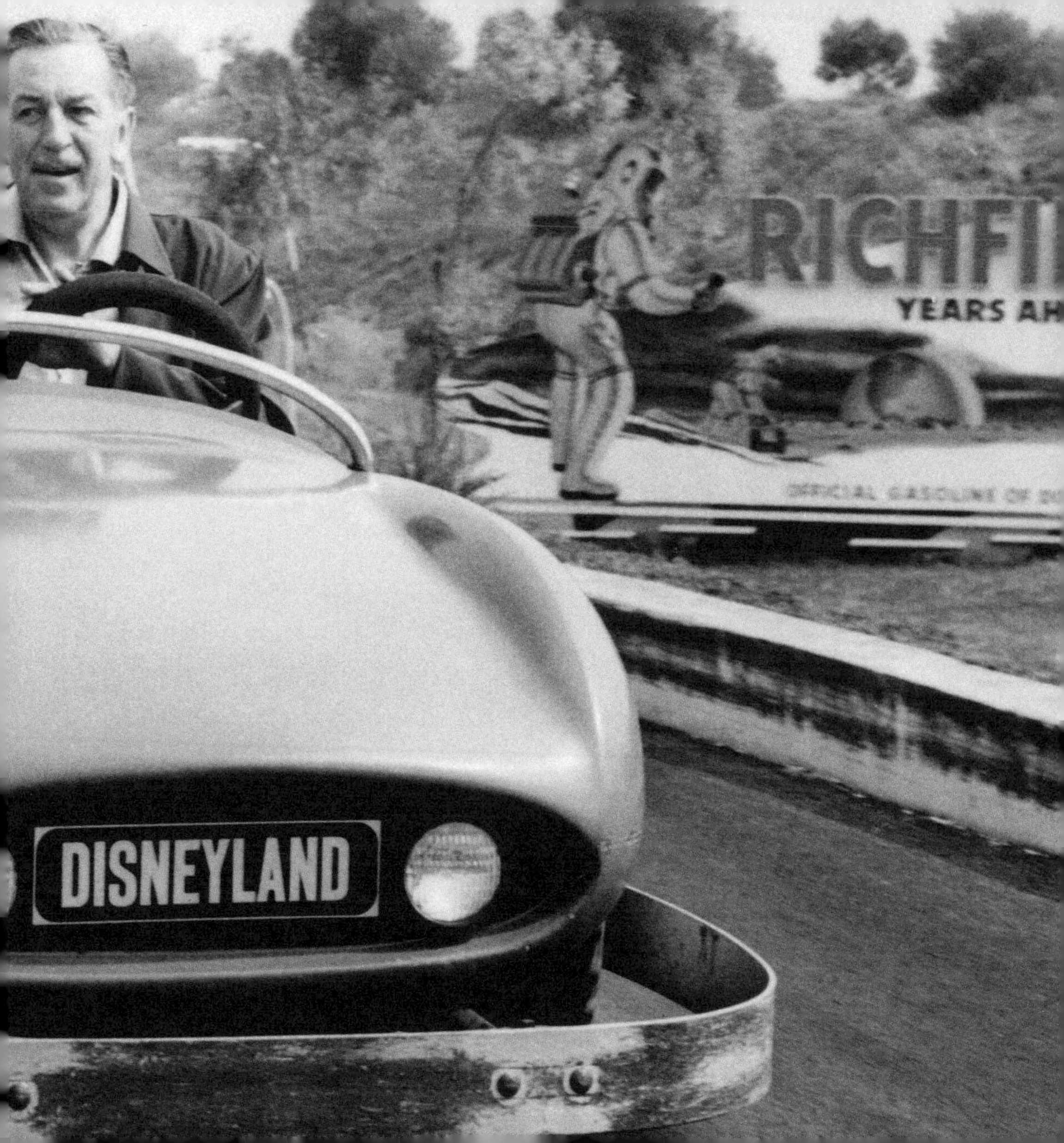
DISNEYLAND

ANNETTE FUNICELLO

ALTHOUGH Walt Disney discovered Annette Funicello's show-stealing abilities during an amateur dance performance in *Swan Lake*, it was her kindergarten teacher who first spotted Annette's toe-tapping sense of rhythm and encouraged her to pick up a musical instrument. Annette didn't need to be asked twice to know what she wanted to play. Before long, she was zealously banging away at the drums with a natural precision, outshining older kids who'd been at it for years.

As the twenty-fourth original Mouseketeer, twelve-year-old Annette may have been the last, but by no stretch of the imagination could she be considered the least. Annette became an instant favorite on *The Mickey Mouse Club*, graduating to best-loved Mouseketeer of all time. By the age of fifteen, Annette regularly received six thousand fan letters each month (not to mention gifts and marriage proposals!).

In spite of all the love and attention she got from her devoted fans, Annette was shy about being different—she wanted blond pigtails, freckles, blue eyes, and a last name that wasn't hard to pronounce. "I want to change my name to Annette Turner," she told Walt Disney one day. Walt did give Annette a name change, but a subtle— and more important—one. He suggested she pronounce her name the proper way, *Fun-i-chell-o*, not *Fun-is-sell-o*, as she'd done her whole life.

When Walt Disney sat in the audience of the Warner Theatre in New York, on October 6, 1927, he experienced an event that would change the face of cinema forever. As he watched the Warner Bros. preview of *The Jazz Singer*, the first film to feature sound, Disney realized that he needed to add this new dimension to his cartoons. He succeeded. On November 18, 1928, *Steamboat Willie* debuted at the Colony Theater in New York and made animation history.

✳ The Buster Keaton films *The Navigator* (1924) and *Steamboat Bill, Jr.* (1928) provided the inspiration for *Steamboat Willie*.

✳ Animator Ub Iwerks completed *Steamboat Willie* as a silent film. Sound was post-synchronized to match the action.

✳ The very first attempt to sync sound with *Steamboat Willie*'s action was a crude one: artist Wilfred Jackson, Iwerks, and Disney played along with a harmonica, washboard, cowbell, frying pan, plumbing tools, and ocarinas.

✳ Disney sold his beloved Moon Cabriolet roadster to finance the recording sessions with New York's Broadway Strand Theater orchestra.

✳ At first, conductor Carl Edouarde found it impossible to coordinate his orchestra with the characters' movements in *Steamboat Willie*. Iwerks solved the problem by making a special print of the film with an animated bouncing ball. The ball bounced along in the rhythms the composer had devised to highlight and punctuate the action. Instead of being projected above the orchestra, Iwerks's special print was projected directly down onto Edouarde's printed score. In this way, Iwerks created a film that could conduct the conductor.

✳ Although Mickey Mouse had already performed high-flying antics in *Plane Crazy* and saved a damsel in distress in *Gallopin' Gaucho*, *Steamboat Willie* came before the public eye first, and is thus considered the first Mickey Mouse cartoon.

THE DISNEY BROTHERS' partnership started as early as 1911, when nine-year-old Walt asked his older brother for a quarter to buy paper on which to draw. Roy backed him, beginning a lifelong pattern of being the financial guru behind Walt's never-ending creativity.

Roy was pragmatic, Walt was a dreamer; Roy was conservative, Walt took risks; Roy knew business, Walt knew art.

ROY O. DISNEY: DREAM MAKER

For all their differences, the Disney brothers made a team like none other.

In 1923 when Walt received an offer for distribution of his Alice Comedies, Roy was laid up in a California hospital with tuberculosis. Walt rushed to see his brother and pleaded for him to "come out and help... get this started." Roy left the hospital the next morning "against medical advice." That day, October 16, Roy and Walt signed a contract and the Walt Disney Company was born.

Forty-three years later, Walt was hospitalized with lung cancer. With Roy at his bedside, Walt mapped out his ultimate fantasy for a prototype community of tomorrow and new "Disneyland East" park. Looking at the ceiling tiles above his hospital bed, Walt mapped out the park section by section.

Walt died the next day, December 15, 1966, but Roy made it his mission to see his brother's dreams come true. He canceled plans for retirement and took full charge of the company at age seventy-three. Production for the "Florida Project" went full speed ahead, and Walt Disney World opened on October 1, 1971. Having granted his brother's last wish, Roy died on December 20.

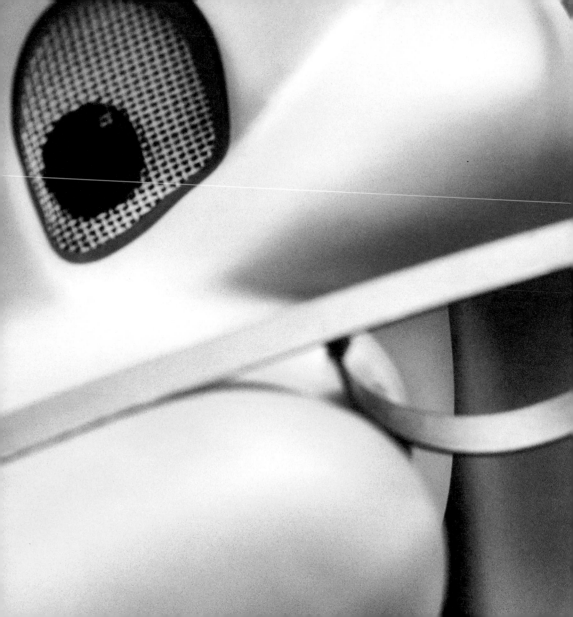

The tradition of Disney topiaries started in 1966 when Disneyland horticulturalists sculpted an array of larger-than-lifesize characters surrounding Fantasyland's It's a Small World. Since then, topiaries have sprung up in all of Disney's parks, as have countless blooming landscapes, making greenery as much a feature of the parks as any ride, exhibit, or show.

* More than 200 topiaries adorn the grounds of Walt Disney World.

* Disneyland and Walt Disney World use different methods for making topiaries. Disneyland cultivates shrubs, which take up to ten years to form; Walt Disney World creates sphagnum-moss topiaries, which take about a month to make.

* Each horticulturalist works on the same topiaries—a change of gardening crew could damage the sculptures.

* One Walt Disney World apatosaurus towering 26 feet high is made up of 8,416 ficus plants.

* Disneyland boasts more than 800 species of plants from more than 40 countries.

* More than 5,000 trees, 40,000 shrubs, and 1 million annuals per year make Disneyland one of the most varied botanical environments in the western United States.

* The 190-acre Tree Farm in Walt Disney World is a growing nursery for thousands of plants, shrubs, trees, and flowers.

* "Edible" landscapes feature apple, lemon, banana, orange, plum, persimmon, avocado, pomegranate, olive, date, fig, and pecan trees, as well as cabbage plants and assorted salad greens.

* The entire landscape seen from the Storybook Land Canal Boats—from buildings to trees—has been sculpted to 1:12 scale.

* Much of the greenery along the Jungle Cruise attraction features plants and trees native to Africa and South America.

* Each spring, the International Flower & Garden Festival at Epcot showcases new topiaries and more than 30 million blooms.

PLEASE
DO NOT FEED
ANIMALS

TRUE-LIFE ADVENTURES

AFTER WORLD WAR II, Walt Disney hired travelogue filmmakers Al and Elma Milotte to film native life in Alaska. The Milottes continually shipped film to Disney, but none of it seemed theater-worthy. Disney planned to scrap the film until a 1947 trip to Alaska inspired an obvious solution—edit out the humans. The result was 27 minutes of seal life on the Pribilof Islands, aptly titled *Seal Island*.

Disney's distributor, RKO, deemed *Seal Island* a hard sell and wanted nothing to do with it. But Disney convinced the Crown Theater in Pasadena to run the film and found that audiences wanted more. Disney announced the short was the first in a new series called *True-Life Adventures*, though at the time, he had no ideas for the next films. *Seal Island* won an Academy Award and RKO agreed to distribute it.

During the next decade, Disney produced a dozen more *True-Life Adventures*. One UCLA doctoral student, N. Paul Kenworthy, Jr., had set up camp in the desert and filmed a wasp who had paralyzed a tarantula to lay her eggs in the stunned arachnid. Disney loved it, and Kenworthy's work became the first series feature, *The Living Desert*. Again, RKO balked. But this time, Roy Disney had a solution: he set up Disney's own distribution arm, Buena Vista Distribution Co. *The Living Desert* raked in $5 million.

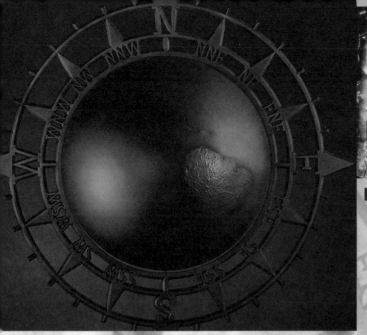

FEATURES

* *The Living Desert* (1953)
* *The Vanishing Prairie* (1954)
  The African Lion (1955)
  Secrets of Life (1956)
* *White Wilderness* (1958)
  Jungle Cat (1960)

FEATURETTES

** *Seal Island* (1949)
** *Beaver Valley* (1950)
** *Nature's Half Acre* (1951)
   The Olympic Elk (1952)
** *Water Birds* (1952)
** *Bear Country* (1953)
   Prowlers of the Everglades (1953)

*Academy Award: Documentary Feature
**Academy Award: Two-Reel Short Subject

WALT DISNEY CUT HIS TEETH on crude animated films in 1920 for the Kansas City Film Ad Co., which promoted banks, hats, and insurance. Dissatisfied with existing material, eighteen-year-old Disney inserted his own gags, to the delight of the company. The eager artist implored his boss to lend him a camera for experimental purposes. His employer said no, but Disney persisted, and soon had the camera at his disposal, toiling away after hours in his studio (formerly the family garage).

By 1922, the success of Newman Laugh-O-grams gave Disney the gumption to quit Film Ad and start his own company, Laugh-O-gram Films. Pictorial Clubs distributors promised to pay $100 deposit plus $11,000 for six fairy tales

LAUGH-O-GRAM FILMS: THE GENESIS

Inspired by Max Fleischer's Out of the Inkwell shorts, Disney worked regularly into the wee hours of the morning. His first film exploited a local problem: the disrepair of Kansas City streets. Disney showed it to the Newman Theatre Company and struck a deal to produce one film per week. Called Newman Laugh-O-grams, the one-minute shorts ran in three theaters.

peppered with gags: *Little Red Riding Hood, The Four Musicians of Bremen, Puss in Boots, Jack and the Beanstalk, Goldie Locks and the Three Bears,* and *Cinderella.* Disney's young animators fulfilled their end of the deal, but Pictorial Clubs didn't. Laugh-O-gram never received another nickel from the distributor after the deposit, forcing Disney to fold the following year.

Did you know? A Kansas City dentist wanting to promote oral hygiene sought the services of Laugh-O-gram Films. Walt Disney couldn't make an appointment because he didn't have the $1.50 necessary to reclaim his only pair of shoes from the cobbler. The dentist paid for Disney's shoes, as well as his first educational film, *Tommy Tucker's Tooth.*

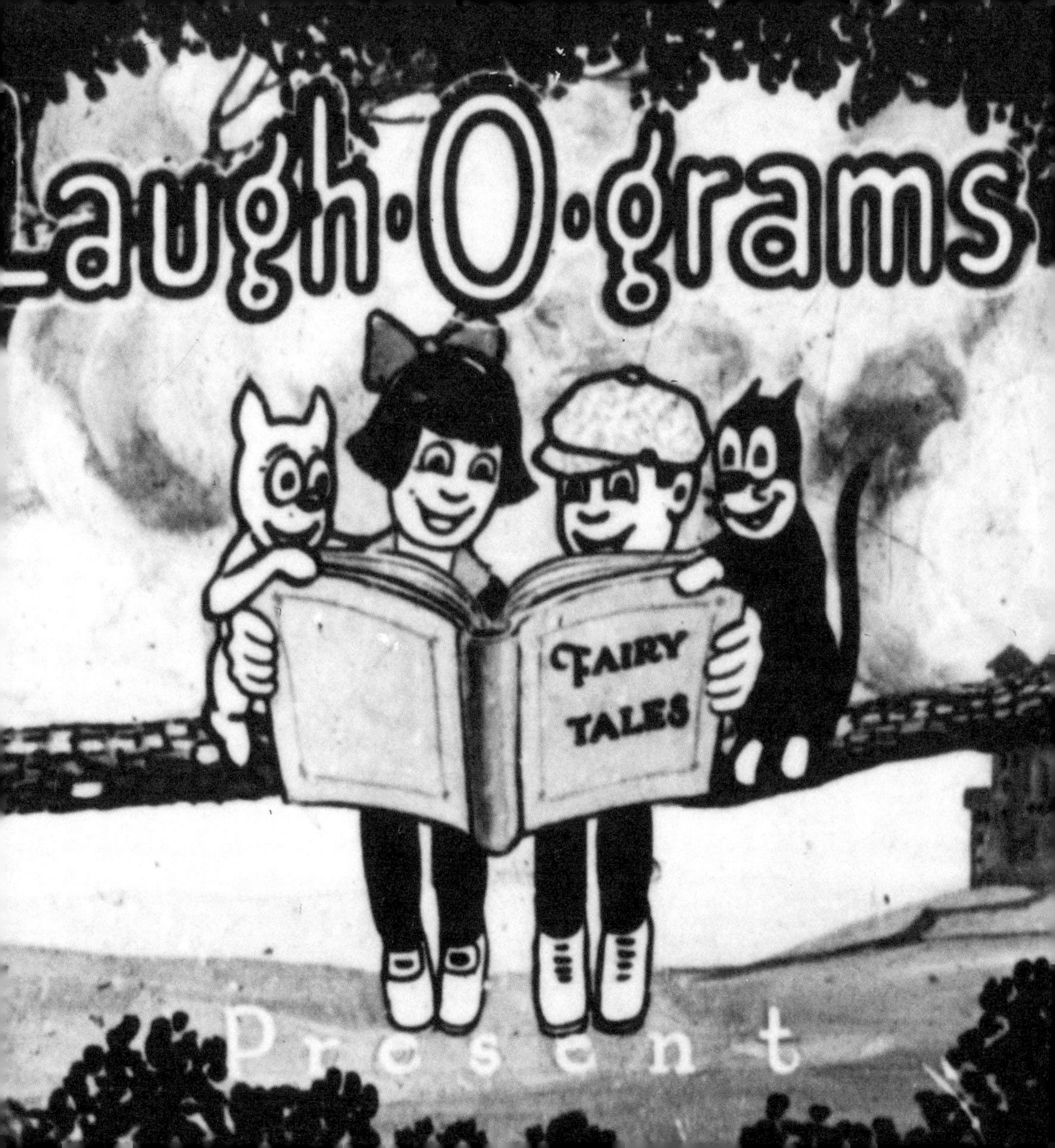
Laugh-O-grams
FAIRY
TALES
Present

MICKEY

On July 30, 1998, *Disney Magic* embarked on her maiden voyage from Port Canaveral, Florida, to Port of Nassau and Disney's Castaway Cay in the Bahamas. Just over a year later, the Disney Cruise Line expanded with the launch of its second ship, *Disney Wonder*, on August 15, 1999. With capacity for 3,345 guests and crew, these 85,000-gross-ton vessels must pack enough power to keep a small village afloat. On any given day aboard these Disney liners:

* 500,000 gallons of fresh water are distilled from sea water

* 280 tons of water drain from the air-conditioning system, 220 tons of which are recycled to operate laundry facilities

* 8,260 cups of coffee are served

* 1,850 telephones are available for phoning home

* diesel storage tanks hold up to 20,000 gallons of fuel

* up to 1.365 megawatts of energy are used to power the ship

* cooks scramble, beat, fry, bake, and hard-boil 5,040 eggs

* 159 quarts of frying oil sizzle on kitchen griddles

* 30 gallons of chocolate ice cream are consumed

* 5,390 pillows cushion sleepy sailors

And what does it take to stop these ships from sailing the Atlantic at a top speed of 24 knots? A 14-ton anchor.

Did you know? Roy Disney took a page from his brother Walt's book when he oversaw the construction of Walt Disney World. Just as Disneyland's Main Street USA honors all those who contributed to its creation by displaying their names on the second-story shop windows, Walt Disney World has a window that features the names of all the holding companies under which the so-called "Florida Project" land purchases were made.

MAIN STREET U.S.A.

DESIGNED TO EXEMPLIFY a turn-of-the-century Midwestern hometown, Main Street U.S.A. represents Walt Disney's desire to capture "America from 1890 to 1910, at the crossroads of an era... [where] the gas lamp is giving way to the electric lamp, and a newcomer, the sputtering 'horseless carriage,' has challenged Old Dobbin for the street-car right-of-way."

Never one to overlook the smallest of details, Disney hired a team of architects, engineers, and artists to recreate a Victorian landscape, from the authentic gaslights and the mansard roofs to historically accurate doorknobs and lettering on shop windows. But that wasn't enough. Disney needed to take his plans one step further to instill the street with a hint of nostalgia and fantasy. He wanted all of Main Street U.S.A. to be at a five-eighths scale. His designers, however, felt this plan would be too extreme, and totally impractical for restaurants and shops. Instead, they opted for a gradual forced perspective, building the first story of all buildings at 90-percent scale, the second story at 80-percent scale, and the third story at 60-percent scale.

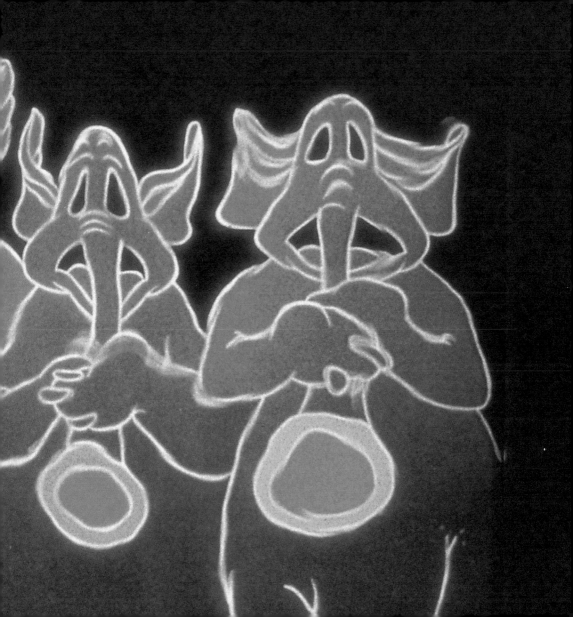

CRUELLA'S HAUTE COUTURE

TO KILL FOR:

* There's no such thing as too much fur.

* Nothing accentuates bold diversity like asymmetrical hair color.

* Explore your wild side with fun patterns—zebra stripes, Siberian tiger, Dalmatian spots.

* Wear your support for endangered animals on your sleeve . . . or lapel. . . or shoes . . . or hat.

* Fur makes every moment of the day luxurious. Even reading in bed is more fun when you're wrapped in fur lingerie.

* Drive a convertible. Show off your fur with style year-round.

* Protect your skin from the elements—wear elbow-length leather gloves at all times. (Of course, they should be lined with fur.)

* Choose accessories that make a statement: A porcupine-quill hat will most definitely get your point across.

* Never, ever mistake a skunk for your purse.

Disneyland's
25 MILLIONTH
VISITOR

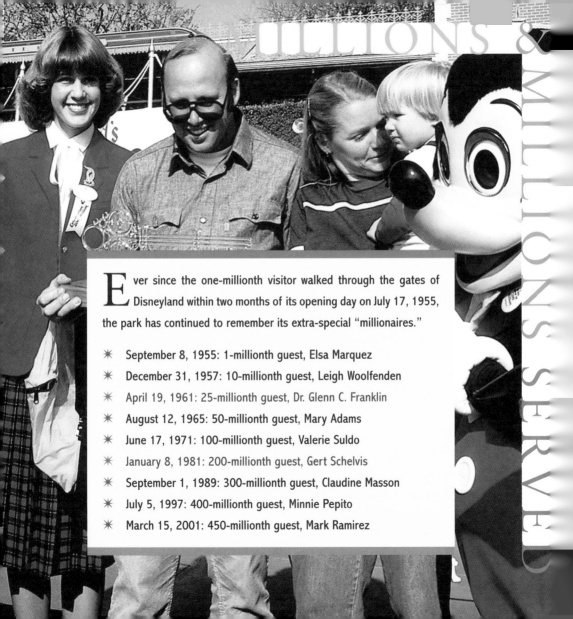

E ver since the one-millionth visitor walked through the gates of Disneyland within two months of its opening day on July 17, 1955, the park has continued to remember its extra-special "millionaires."

✳ September 8, 1955: 1-millionth guest, Elsa Marquez

✳ December 31, 1957: 10-millionth guest, Leigh Woolfenden

✳ April 19, 1961: 25-millionth guest, Dr. Glenn C. Franklin

✳ August 12, 1965: 50-millionth guest, Mary Adams

✳ June 17, 1971: 100-millionth guest, Valerie Suldo

✳ January 8, 1981: 200-millionth guest, Gert Schelvis

✳ September 1, 1989: 300-millionth guest, Claudine Masson

✳ July 5, 1997: 400-millionth guest, Minnie Pepito

✳ March 15, 2001: 450-millionth guest, Mark Ramirez

Winchell's television career lasted through the late 1960s, during which time he expanded his creative repertoire into voice talent and inventing. As a child, Winchell had wanted to be an artist or a doctor and his most significant invention reflected both ideals. In the mid-1950s, Winchell observed thoracic surgeries performed by Dr. Henry Heimlich (who later invented the Heimlich maneuver)

PAUL WINCHELL: LIFE IN STRIPES

HE COINED TIGGER'S signature sign-off, "Ta-ta for now," and remained the distinguished voice of the Hundred-Acre Wood feline for more than thirty years. Prior to that, Paul Winchell spent his life bouncing ideas—and voices—around.

Winchell got his start in show biz at fourteen, with a ventriloquism act on the *Major Bowes Amateur Hour* radio show. Even though listening audiences couldn't see his dummies, Winchell's comedy routines came through loud and clear, bringing in record telephone votes and earning him fifty dollars per week in 1937. Ten years later Winchell and his dummy gained a viewing audience on television with *The Paul Winchell–Jerry Mahoney Show.*

and became inspired to create an artificial heart. He created a prototype and received a patent for his innovation, which he donated to the University of Utah. In 1969, Winchell's model became the first artificial heart used to sustain a patient's life.

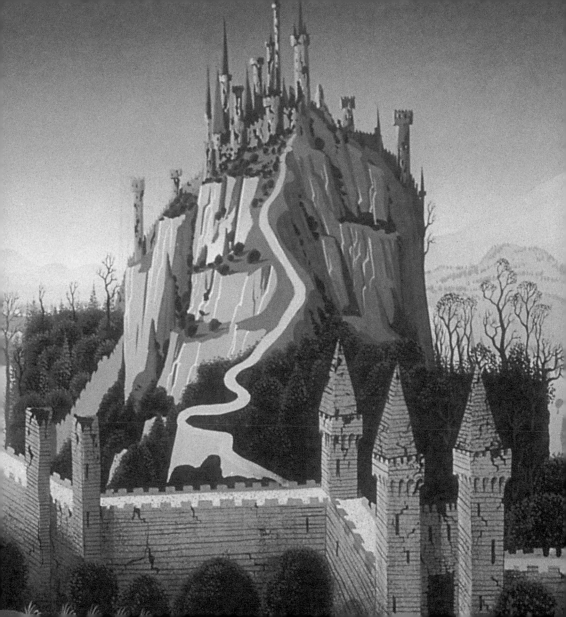

MILT KAHL

MARC DAVIS

FRANK THOMAS

WOLFGANG "WOOLIE" REITHERMAN

LES CLARK

44

ERIC LARSON

OLLIE JOHNSTON

JOHN LOUNSBERY

WARD KIMBALL

In 1940, the Disney Studio started a new era with its move to Burbank, California. Among the changes, the animators created the Animation Board as a way to hire, train, and manage personnel in their department. For ten years, board members changed regularly, but by 1950, the core group of supervising animators became a permanent fixture at the studio. In jest, Walt Disney compared the board to Franklin D. Roosevelt's Supreme Court justices, who the president had dubbed "the Nine Old Men." Although most of the animators were still in their thirties, the name stuck.

THE YEAR 1932 ushered in a new era of Disney films: color. Disney's staff exploded from 125 to well into the thousands by the middle of the decade. The advent of color also necessitated an entirely new department: Ink and Paint.

Inkers and painters had the painstaking jobs of tracing the animators' drawings onto celluloid, painting carefully selected colors onto the back of every cel, and applying special

THE INK & PAINT GIRLS

effects and colors to the front of every cel. Disney felt that such highly detailed work required the patience and neatness of a woman. Thus, the Ink and Paint Department became the only division open exclusively to women artists.

During the production of the 1937 feature *Snow White and the Seven Dwarfs,* 244 inkers and painters completed 21 to 28 cels each per day, or approximately 250,000 cels for the entire film. Many of the women decided that Snow White's hair looked too harsh for her fair complexion and took innovative liberties to soften her features, adding gray highlights to her hair and rouge to her cheeks. Disney questioned whether they would be able to maintain consistency within each cel, but the girls assuaged his fears, claiming they had plenty of practice applying makeup.

The Ink and Paint girls remained a vital part of the animation process well into the 1950s and beyond, although in lesser numbers. The adaption of a Xerox copying process to animation in 1959 mechanized the transfer of animators' drawings to celluloid. Today, virtually all inking and painting is computerized.

DREAMY SONGS

From a wish on a star to a dream come true, such sentiments have been the ingredients of many a Disney song. Test your music memory and match the songs below with their films:

1. "When You Wish Upon a Star"

2. "A Dream Is a Wish Your Heart Makes"

3. "The Second Star to the Right"

4. "Once Upon a Dream"

5. "I'm Wishing"

6. "My Favorite Dream"

7. "The Wishing Song"

8. "A Man Has Dreams"

9. "A Star Is Born"

10. "Part of Your World"

a. Cinderella

b. Snow White and the Seven Dwarfs

c. Darby O'Gill and the Little People

d. Pinocchio

e. Mary Poppins

f. Sleeping Beauty

g. Hercules

h. Fun and Fancy Free

i. Peter Pan

j. The Little Mermaid

48

Answers on p. 352

JOHN HENCH: LIFER

WORKING MORE THAN SIXTY years with the Walt Disney Company, John Hench rightfully earned the moniker *lifer*. Hench started his Disney career as a story artist in 1939. He did everything from background and layout to art direction, effects animation, and special effects. Having gained Disney's respect as one of the Studio's most gifted artists, Hench teamed up with Salvador Dali in 1946 on the never completed film *Destino*. In 1954, Hench's lead development of the hydraulic giant squid in *20,000 Leagues Under the Sea* helped earn the film an Academy Award for Best Special Effects.

From the studio, Hench joined WED Enterprises, later known as Walt Disney Imagineering, to design attractions for Disneyland and eventually every subsequent Disney theme park to date. His creative endeavors have made an impact beyond Disney borders; the well-known torches of the Olympic Games are modeled after Hench's designs for the 1960 Winter Olympics at Squaw Valley, California.

In addition to his pioneering contributions to Disney films and parks, Hench has been the official portrait artist for Mickey Mouse. In 1990, Michael Eisner presented Hench with the Disney Legend award.

Did you know? John Hench did not like working on *Fantasia's* "Nutcracker Suite." When he asked Walt Disney for a new assignment, Disney responded with backstage passes to an entire season of ballet. Thereafter, Hench admittedly learned something about dance and continued with the segment "quite willingly."

INSTRUCTOR

GOOFY

From 1941 to 1957, the gangly, good-natured Goofy tried to impart his wisdom in several "How to" films and television shows, only to discover he never quite got it right himself.

How to Ride a Horse

How to Play Baseball

How to Swim

How to Fish

How to Be a Sailor

How to Play Golf

How to Play Football

How to Be a Detective

How to Dance

How to Sleep

How to Relax

Did you know? Goofy debuted as a nameless audience member in the 1932 short *Mickey's Revue*. By the mid '30s the affable canine appeared in newspaper cartoon strips as Dippy Dawg. The 1938 publication of *The Story of Dippy the Goof* hinted at the character's new identity, but it wasn't until the cartoon release of *Goofy and Wilbur* in 1939, that the name Goofy finally stuck.

PASSAMAQUODDY

WHEN THE DISNEY STUDIO made plans to tell the story of a good-natured dragon who inadvertently wreaks havoc in a small Maine fishing village, studio executives found their $10 million budget insufficient for a Maine shoot. The logical solution: build a new town.

Oscar-winning art director Jack Martin Smith, known for *Cleopatra*, *Fantastic Voyage,* and *Hello, Dolly!*, spent $250,000 to create the fictional town of Passamaquoddy from scratch on the back lot of the Disney Studio. He organized the face-lift of thirty existing buildings on the studio's Western Street, the construction of eight additional ones, and the installation of a special concrete-lined pool to accommodate the period fishing boats and docks of the seaside village.

Smith's coup: a 52-foot lighthouse built on Point Buchon, a promontory south of Morro Bay, California. Although it overlooks the Pacific Ocean, the area's brisk winds and stunning view resemble the northeastern United States coast. At a cost of $115,000, the lighthouse took fifty men three weeks to build. Upon completion of the film, some talk circulated about preserving the lighthouse as part of an attraction for Disneyland or Walt Disney World. The plans never came to fruition, and the top of the lighthouse sat on the Burbank back lot for several years before finally deteriorating beyond repair.

Did you know? The lighthouse lamp in *Pete's Dragon* shone so bright that the film's location manager needed to obtain special permission from the Coast Guard to light it for filming. The lamp, with its $6,000 Fresnell-type lens, could cast a beacon eighteen to twenty-four miles— far enough to confuse passing ships.

CARL BARKS, THE ARTIST who gave the world Scrooge McDuck, the Beagle Boys, Gladstone Gander,

CARL BARKS: DUCKBURG'S FOUNDING FATHER

Magica de Spell, and a host of other Duckburg characters, is a comic artist of international renown.

Born in 1901, Barks took up drawing at an early age. Although he had aspired to become a cartoonist, he spent much of his youth and early adulthood doing a host of hard-labor jobs, including working on his parents' grain ranch, logging, and toiling on a riveting gang.

Barks's first break in the art world came in 1928, when he started selling cartoons to the Minneapolis periodical *Calgary Eye-Opener*. He continued doing odd jobs until 1935, when he learned of an opening at the Disney studio, and applied. Barks joined the animation department, and soon after devised a brilliant barber's-chair gag for Donald Duck in the short *Modern Inventions* (1937). He earned fifty dollars for his work and a promotion to the story department, where he would work for seven years.

During the war years when Disney turned the studio into a military training film center, Barks lost interest in the projects. He left Disney in 1942 to start a chicken farm with his wife and take up freelance cartooning. He quickly landed work with a Disney licensee, Western Publishing. Starting with "Donald Duck Finds Pirate Gold," Barks scripted, penciled, and inked Donald Duck comics until he retired in 1966.

But Barks didn't stop. He merely traded his pen for a brush and painted dozens of oil paintings and watercolors of his famous Duckburg residents. The paintings have sold for hundreds of thousands of dollars to collectors—a testament of his ability to appeal to adult sensibilities as well as children's.

Inspired by the novels *The Magic Bed-Knob* and *Bonfires and Broomsticks* by British author Mary Norton, the 1971 feature *Bedknobs and Broomsticks* is a witch's brew of three orphans, one apprentice spell-caster, a con man, a legendary island, and a flying bed. The concoction worked well enough to fend off invading Germans from the coastal village of Pepperinge Eye. Some notable facts:

* The film earned an Academy Award for Best Special Visual Effects as well as garnered nominations in four other categories: Best Song, Best Score, Best Costume Design, and Best Art/Set Direction.

* Plans for the film dated back more than a decade from its release; at one time Walt Disney considered completing production of *Bedknobs* before *Mary Poppins* (1964).

* The journey portrayed in *Bedknobs and Broomsticks* was not the first time Angela Lansbury fled wartime London. During World War II, she made it on the last boat alongside her mother and brothers to be evacuated from London to the United States.

* The army enchanted with substitutiary locomotion experienced an afterlife in the Warner Bros. musical *Camelot*.

* The Sherman brothers started writing the score in 1964. Box office reviews led the Disney studio to cut the film from 117 to 98 minutes—most of the cuts were music. But in 1996, for the film's twenty-fifth anniversary, the studio released *Bedknobs* with twenty-four extra minutes. This original footage included fully restored songs and two additional ones, "With a Flair" and "Nobody's Problems for Me."

* Director of animation Ward Kimball gave a nod to the company's legacy: during the King's football match on the isle of Naboombu, a flag-waving bear in the back row of the stadium is sporting a Mickey Mouse T-shirt.

ISLE OF NABOOMBU

THE FIRST CAST MEMBER

ALTHOUGH DISNEYLAND didn't open until July 1955, legend has it that Walt Disney made his first purchase of livestock for his future "Mickey Mouse Park" in 1953. Walt bought a little Sardinian donkey named Picolino, which he kept at his niece's house until the animal's first day on the job. Eager to celebrate the momentous event, Walt commissioned Herb Ryman, one of his top art directors and designers, to paint a portrait of the beloved beast.

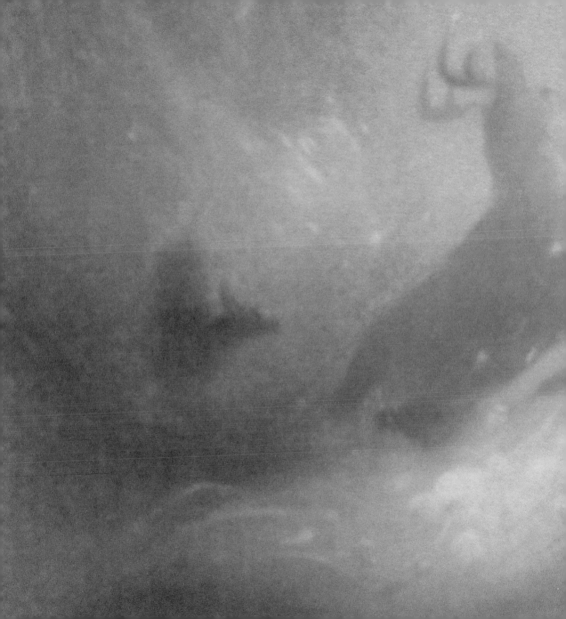

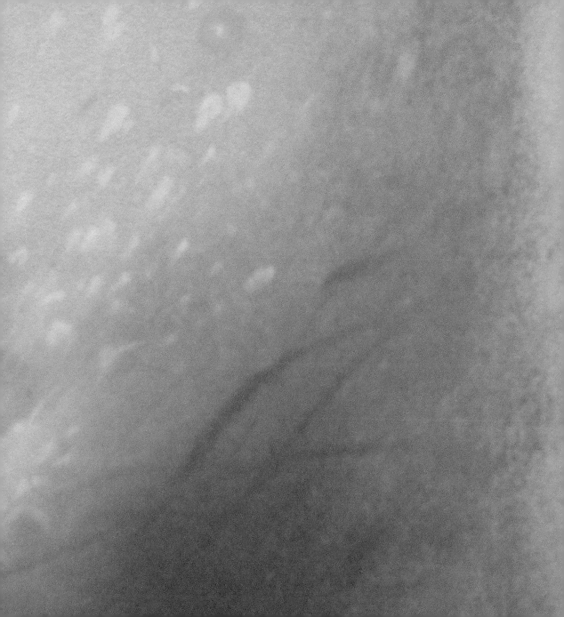

DISNEY'S ANIMAL KINGDOM

Earth Day 1998 saw the opening of Disney's Animal Kingdom. Its varied environmental habitats circle the Tree of Life, the park's central spectacular feature. Covering more than 500 acres, this "new species of theme park" is home to:

* more than 4 million plants from around the globe

* the capybara, the world's largest rodent

* giraffes Zari and Miles, the first animals to take up residence in the park

* the secretary bird, a large African bird of prey that feeds largely on snakes

* 94 acres of fields cultivated specially for a variety of favorite animal snack foods, including acacia, banana, papaya, palm, and willow

* the giant anteater, which devours more than 10 pounds of ants daily

* DinoLand, U.S.A., whose plant and animal inhabitants have relatives that lived with the dinosaurs

* eyelash-batting birds such as the red-legged seriemas and the ostrich

* bamboo, the world's fastest-growing plant, which can gain 2 inches of height per hour

* *Cuphea llavea*, the purple-and-red blooming shrub nicknamed "the Mickey Mouse plant" because of its big-eared blossoms

RENOWNED for flat, 2-D, static compositions, Mary Blair had a style like no one else's. Her unconventional colors and shapes inspired as well as frustrated Disney artists for more than thirty years. When asked to bring her concept paintings and gouaches to life, Disney animators couldn't add dimension and movement to them without losing the essence of Mary's art in the translation.

Mary had achieved success as a member of the California School of Watercolor in the 1930s, but the Depression forced her to compromise her ideals as a fine artist for the more lucrative path of animation art. By 1940, she had landed a job with Walt Disney, and quickly won his heart. When the U.S. government asked Walt to tour South America as part of its "Good Neighbor" policy, Walt included Mary among eighteen others to go on the trip. The summer of '41 made an immeasurable impact on Mary's art. Her palette exploded with colors as never before. Of the films that Walt Disney produced as a direct result of that trip, *Saludos Amigos* and *The Three Caballeros* are distinctly Blair.

Although Mary provided countless paintings and sketches for animated features such as *Cinderella*, *Alice in Wonderland*, and *Peter Pan*, most of them never made it to the final cut untouched. Determined to give Mary a showcase of her own, Walt asked her to design a boat-ride exhibit for the 1964 World's Fair. *It's a Small World* consequently was born on an airplane when Mary sketched a clock tower on a scrap of paper. Mary's handcrafted exhibits that remain on permanent display at Disneyland and Walt Disney World are perhaps the most faithful renditions of her art in 3-D form.

MARY BLAIR

DISNEYLAND'S HAUNTED MANSION remained a mystery for ten years before the attraction officially opened on August 9, 1969. For years, Walt Disney and his creative team tossed around ideas for the inside of the stately southern manor. Disney Imagineers built three different models, ranging from a menacing exterior that looked in constant need of repair, to the idyllic antebellum mansion that appears in the parks today. Disney insisted that the building's exterior look clean and attractive, fitting in with the rest of the architecture in Disneyland's New Orleans Square. The haunting would be restricted to the inside of the mansion.

Developing the look of the Haunted Mansion proved to be the first of many hurdles in the planning process. The build-

HAUNTED SPIRITS

ing went up in 1963, but the question lingered: How will people go through the mansion? Some plans called for guests to walk through

the spirited house, but Disney feared that might cause too much congestion and abandoned the idea. Ultimately, Imagineers devised doom buggies that transport guests—along with hitchhiking ghosts—through the attraction.

The Haunted Mansion, filled with 999 happy but ghoulish spirits, proved to be a unique technical challenge to Disney Imagineers. The combination of Audio-Animatronics and special effects represented one of the most complex exhibits Disney artists had designed to date. When the attraction first opened, live actors "haunted" the mansion as well, posing in suits of armor, to offer a frightening welcome.

Nearly half a century after the opening of Disneyland, The Walt Disney Company expanded its theme-park presence in the nation's Golden State with a 55-acre park dedicated to the history and mystique of the California dream. Disney's California Adventure offers entertainment, lore, and palate-pleasing delectables in three themed districts. Some highlights:

GOLDEN STATE

Celebrate California's natural beauty and cultural diversity of its people.

* Thrill seekers can white-knuckle it down the hairiest white-water rafting ride, Grizzly River Run.

* Gourmands can sink their teeth into the famous sourdough bread of San Francisco, as well as sample hundreds of fruits and vegetables at Bountiful Valley Farm.

* Fly high above the wonders of the Golden State in Soarin' Over California, a realistic free flight experience.

PARADISE PIER

Inspired by classic seaside amusement parks, this is the hot spot for high-speed roller coasters and midway games.

* Be catapulted skyward 180 feet in only two minutes; then bounce back bungee-like on the Maliboomer.

* The California Screamin' roller coaster sends guests through several scream tunnels before looping around Mickey's head.

* The 150-foot ride-within-a-ride Sun Wheel takes center stage along the pier. Passengers can view the entire park across the four-acre bay.

HOLLYWOOD PICTURES BACKLOT

Stargazers can go "on location" and enjoy the world of celebrity madness on this motion picture studio "lot."

* ABC Soap Opera Bistro has the real dish for soap lovers. Dine in Port Charles, at General Hospital, or with All My Children and get served by playboys, amnesia victims, or good and evil twins.

* Stroll down Hollywood Boulevard and take in the scene, pop into Disney Animation for exhibits and demonstrations.

77

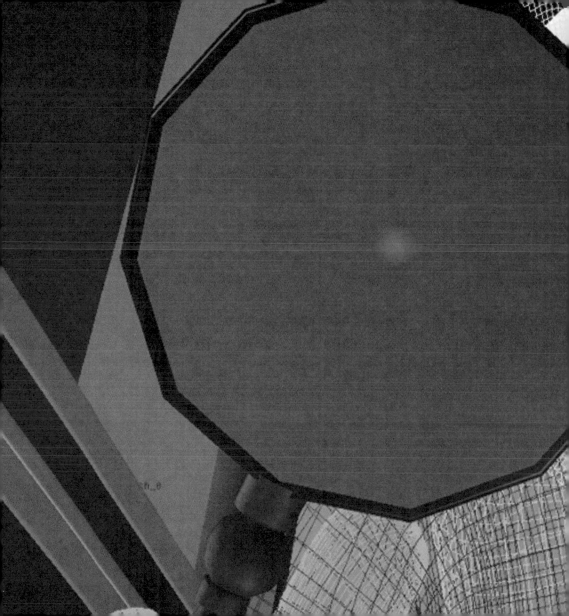

Age: 32

BIRTHPLACE: Fishkill, New York

EDUCATION:
Oxford University (1896-1903)
Double Doctorate in Linguistic
Theory (grammatical structure,
syntax, babel theory, evolution,
written languages, and lost
alphabets) and Dead Languages
(cryptology and hieroglyphics,
with thesis work done on American
Indian tribes of the California
Coast, Hawaiian, Pacific Islands,
and South Asian Sub-Continent).
Minor Degrees in Chemistry,
Literature (French, Old English,
Chinese), Art History, Sociology,
and Anthropology

Tutored by the legendary Thaddeus
Thatch (paternal grandfather) in
the fields of cartography, draft-
ing, navigation, astronomy,
archaeology, and antique restoration techniques.

EMPLOYMENT:
Museum Linguist/Translator and
Cartographic Restoration Expert,
Washington D.C., May 21,
1903-1914.
Participated in Academic Exchange
Program 1909-1910; spent eleven
months working in Paris at the
Bibliothèque Nationale and the
Prado Museum in Madrid.

BACKGROUND:
Orphaned by a railway accident in
1885, Milo Thatch was raised and
educated by his grandfather
Thaddeus Thatch. Milo took after
his grandfather in his affinity
and passion for languages and
antiquities. Graduated Buford
Beaumont High School at age
eleven, accepted (and declined)
admission at Harvard, Yale, and
Princeton Universities, 1895.
Enrolled at Oxford University,
1896. Tried out for Rowing Team
1899 (rejected), Archery Team
1900 (rejected), Debating Team
1900 (accepted), Cricket Team
1901 (rejected), and Chess Team
1902 (accepted). Despite his
expertise and accomplishments,
Milo is rumored to have been
employed primarily because of hi
relationship to Thaddeus Thatch.
Occasionally tutors Georgetown
students in literature and art
history to supplement his income
Was briefly involved (22 days)
with a Miss Lisa McGrath, Janua
1905. No subsequent or current
girlfriends or romantic attach-
ments known. Currently resides
Twinbrook, Maryland, with a lon
hair Persian cat (Fluffy) and h
extensive library.

COAST OF IRELAND

THE UNEXPECTED RUNAWAY success of *Steamboat Willie* (1928) turned Mickey Mouse into an overnight icon. By 1930, fifteen shorts had been released across the country and Mickey Mouse merchandise from buttons to books had found its way into millions of homes.

The Disney brothers remained extremely cautious about protecting their creation against infringement. Nevertheless, the popularity of the Mouse grew, as did unlicensed Mickey Mouse merchandise. One such item came to life in 1930 at the hands of Charlotte Clark, a Burbank, California, woman. Clark wanted to make a Mickey that children could hold. She asked her fourteen-year-old nephew, Bob Clampett, to make a sketch of the Mouse as

Walt and Roy immediately rented a house near the Disney Studio for Clark and eight others to produce her dolls. The homey factory quickly became dubbed "The

CHARLOTTE CLARK'S DOLL HOUSE

a pattern for a stuffed doll. Clampett spent many hours in the theaters watching Mickey Mouse cartoons until he had enough drawings for his aunt. Clark made her doll, and was so pleased, she showed the Disneys. Their response couldn't have been more enthusiastic.

Doll House." Before the end of the year, The Doll House was stuffing and sewing up to four hundred dolls each week.

Charlotte Clark dolls sold for a whopping $4.95, a steep price to pay during the Depression. By 1932, Walt devised a way to make them more affordable—he released the design to *McCalls* magazine, which thereafter sold Mickey Mouse pattern #91 to the general public for ten cents.

FOR OPTIMUM HEALTH AND HAPPINESS OF YOUR PETS:

* Always keep a friendly fire in the hearth.

* Include your pets in your work. Confer with them about important decisions.

* Dance with them. If you have a fish, swirl the water so she can dance, too.

* If you bring a new pet— or puppet—into the house, make sure to introduce them properly.

* If you suspect your pets may be jealous of newcomers, reassure them that they shouldn't worry.

* Flatter your fish with pet names like "my little water baby."

* Encourage your pets to love each other and kiss good night.

* Make sure your pet has a special place to sleep at night, but leave a little extra room in your own bed just in case.

* Have meals together.

* When traveling, take your animals with you.

* And no matter how absentminded you may be, avoid putting fires out in the fishbowl.

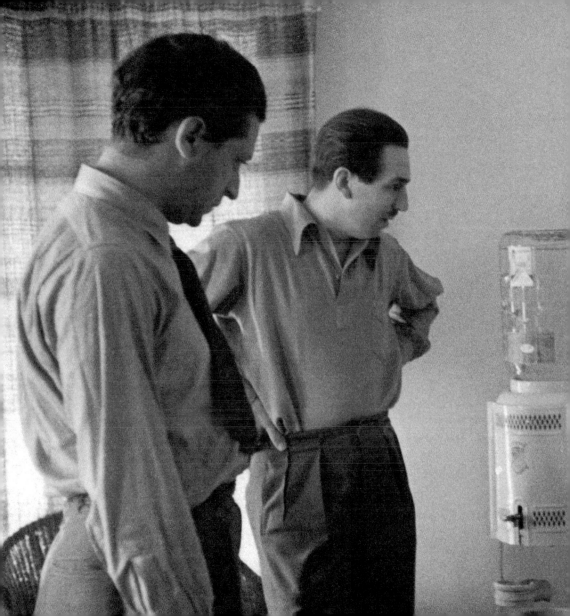

When *THE LOVE BUG* debuted in 1969, it struck a chord in American pop culture. Owing to its flower-power references and the mass appeal of the not-so-chic but ever-so-loved Bug, moviegoers flocked to see the antics of the mischievous Volkswagen Beetle named Herbie. The comedy, based on Gordon Buford's story "Car-Boy-Girl," became the highest grossing film of the year, reaping nearly $60 million within the first few months of its release.

Herbie gained a cult following. Hundreds of beetle owners drove their adorned VWs through the gates of Disneyland for Love Bug Day in celebration of the film. Legions more Herbiefied their cars with "53" decals and red, white, and blue stripes. Meanwhile, for those too young to drive, "love bug" became a favorite backseat car game. Every time players spotted a VW beetle, they shouted "Love bug!" and punched their opponents in the arm for points.

THE LOVE BUG

The Love Bug's success sparked numerous sequels: *Herbie Rides Again* (1974), *Herbie Goes to Monte Carlo* (1977), and *Herbie Goes Bananas*, (1980), as well as the television series *Herbie, the Love Bug* (1982). In 1999, Walt Disney World's All-Star Movies resort opened two Love Bug buildings solely dedicated to Herbie. The Love Bug's popularity still continues with fan clubs, collectibles, and even a look-alike appearance on a 2000 cover of *VW Trends* magazine. A new movie starring Herbie will be released in the summer of 2002.

Did you know? In the scenes in which Herbie the Love Bug appears to be driving, the spunky Beetle actually had help from a backseat driver... and a second steering wheel. The real driver looked through a hole cut out of the VW's floor to see where he was going.

Fill in the blanks with the corresponding nonsensical song titles from Disney's films.

SOLVING TIP: Hyphens and spaces are omitted from all answers.

ACROSS

1. The wise owl's words in Jeremiah's scrapbook.
4. South of the border with Joe, Panchito, and Donald.
6. What a day for Little John and Robin Hood.
7. A flirting lesson for Millionaire Cordelia Drexel Biddle.
8. A Jabberwocky start.
9. Merlin's magic words.

DOWN

2. Donald's samba.
3. Snow White's washing song.
5. Canine lullaby.

Answers on p. 352

THE SUPERCALIFRAGILISTIC-EXPIALIDOCIOUS SHERMAN BROTHERS

IF IT HADN'T BEEN for a dare, more than 200 infectious melodies written by the Sherman brothers may never have existed. Sons of Depression-era songwriter Al Sherman, Robert and Richard never envisioned themselves following in their father's footsteps. In the late 1940s, their father said the struggling brothers couldn't collaborate on a song a kid would spend a nickel on. A decade later, they proved their father wrong.

In 1958, they cowrote "Tall Paul (He's My All)." Annette Funicello recorded it, and the single sold 700,000 copies. Before long, the Shermans were pumping out tunes for Disney's television movies and feature films. But their Academy Award–winning work on *Mary Poppins* started much earlier—in Robert and Richard's childhood. Memories of taking medicine "with a spoonful of sugar" or flying kites with their father inspired many of the film's songs. Even the nonsense words they made up, such as *supercalifragilisticexpialidocious*, came in handy.

One song the Sherman brothers never dreamed would become popular was a simple ditty they wrote for a 1964 World's Fair attraction. They considered donating their royalties to charity. "Don't you ever do that!" Disney chided when they told him. "This song is gonna see your kids through college. Make a donation...but don't give away your royalties." Two years later, Disney made his point when he moved "It's a Small World" permanently to Disneyland.

97

1. Of course, you must be born into nobility (like us), live on a wealthy estate (like us), and have a mother who wants nothing more than to further your interests (like ours).

2. Start the day as any princess would—with breakfast in bed.

3. Take time to engage in the musical arts.

4. Discard old clothing and jewelry in favor of new, more expensive items.

5. Don't fraternize with household help.

6. Accept ALL invitations to Royal Balls.

7. Wear colors that are fresh and flattering—our personal favorites are Avocado and Eggplant.

8. Take every opportunity to see who's who in social settings (even if it means butting through crowds).

9. When presenting feet to royalty for royal shoe fittings, it's always best to take matters into your own hands.

10. And, most importantly, flaunt your noble status proudly—you're entitled!

MAIN STREET ELECTRICAL PARADE

THE DISNEYLAND Main Street Electrical Parade became an instant sensation on June 17, 1972. Over the course of 3,600 runs, the 700,000-bulb spectacle had dazzled more than 75 million people. Most park attractions retire quietly to make way for new events, but the Main Street Electrical parade needed to extend its run an additional five weeks until November 25, 1996, to meet public demand. Although new events now trumpet through Disneyland, the Electrical Parade's 26-unit procession marches on to the synthesized tunes of "Baroque Hoedown" along Walt Disney World's Main Street and Disneyland Paris.

WALT DISNEY LEARNED a hard lesson in 1928 when he lost the rights to his first character, Oswald the Lucky Rabbit. Thereafter, he vowed to retain the rights to all of his creative properties. So, in 1936, when the time came to renew his distribution contract with United Artists, the clause pertaining to television rights prevented him from picking up his pen. UA wanted to retain the rights, but Disney walked away—a decision that would help launch the Walt Disney Company into a new dimension two decades later.

Disney's first foray into the medium was in 1944 with RCA. *The World in Your Living Room* spot sought to educate the public about the benefits of television. The show never aired, but proved to be invaluable homework. His appetite whetted, Disney commissioned the C. J. LaRoche research firm to assess the financial pros and cons of television production. The report: Give it a trial run.

TELEVISION: THE NEW MEDIUM

On December 25, 1950, at 4 P.M., Disney entered the TV age with *One Hour in Wonderland,* on NBC. A staggering 20 million viewers watched, equaling 90 percent of America's 10.5 million television-owning households.

In 1953, deep in debt and in need of money to finance his ultimate dream park, Disney saw TV as a publicity vehicle—and a means to an end. ABC agreed to a seven-year contract in exchange for financial backing of Disneyland. Disney announced plans for his weekly show to the horror of Hollywood producers, who decried it as the death of show biz. But he ignored the critics; *Disneyland* aired October 27, 1954. The variety series introduced Disney's theme park to the public, and broadcast documentaries, shorts, cartoons, and the Emmy Award–winning mini-series *Davy Crockett.*

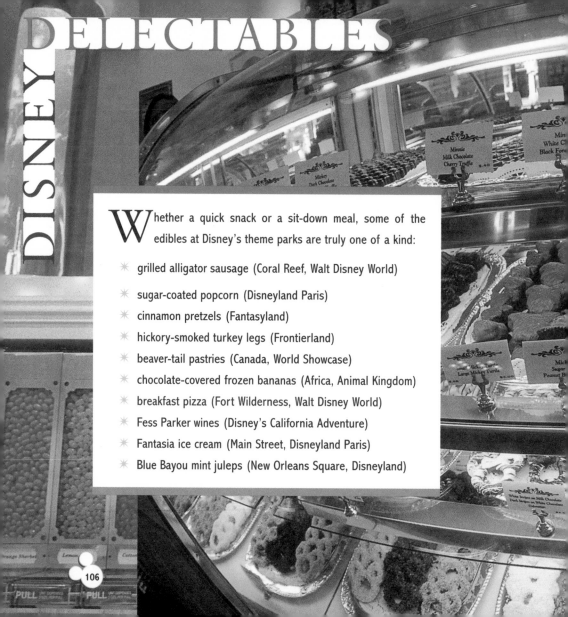

Whether a quick snack or a sit-down meal, some of the edibles at Disney's theme parks are truly one of a kind:

* grilled alligator sausage (Coral Reef, Walt Disney World)

* sugar-coated popcorn (Disneyland Paris)

* cinnamon pretzels (Fantasyland)

* hickory-smoked turkey legs (Frontierland)

* beaver-tail pastries (Canada, World Showcase)

* chocolate-covered frozen bananas (Africa, Animal Kingdom)

* breakfast pizza (Fort Wilderness, Walt Disney World)

* Fess Parker wines (Disney's California Adventure)

* Fantasia ice cream (Main Street, Disneyland Paris)

* Blue Bayou mint juleps (New Orleans Square, Disneyland)

Edible Mickeys

Rice Krispies™ treats

PB&Js

fried cheese

waffles

pretzels

ice-cream bars

chicken nuggets

pasta

pancakes

PERHAPS THE MOST familiar face in Frontierland's Grizzly Hall is the melancholic bear known as Big Al. Although Big Al made his debut in Florida at Walt Disney World on October 1, 1971, he was originally supposed to star with his nineteen life-size Audio-Animatronic cohorts on the West Coast as early as 1966—but not at Disneyland. Walt Disney had intentions of buying land in the Sierra Nevada mountain town of Mineral King, California, for a ski resort, but Congress voted to turn that land into part of Sequoia National Park, preventing any private development.

BIG AL

Big Al is a tribute to the late Imagineer Al Bertino, who was responsible for writing and animating nineteen shorts from some in *Make Mine Music* in 1946 to the Warner Brothers' Road Runner/Wile E. Coyote cartoon *Highway Runnery*, in 1965. Disney artist Marc Davis used Bertino as a model for the creation of Big Al, whose doleful performance of *Blood on the Saddle*, voiced by Hollywood cowboy star Tex Ritter, has become one of the hallmarks of the Country Bear Jamboree.

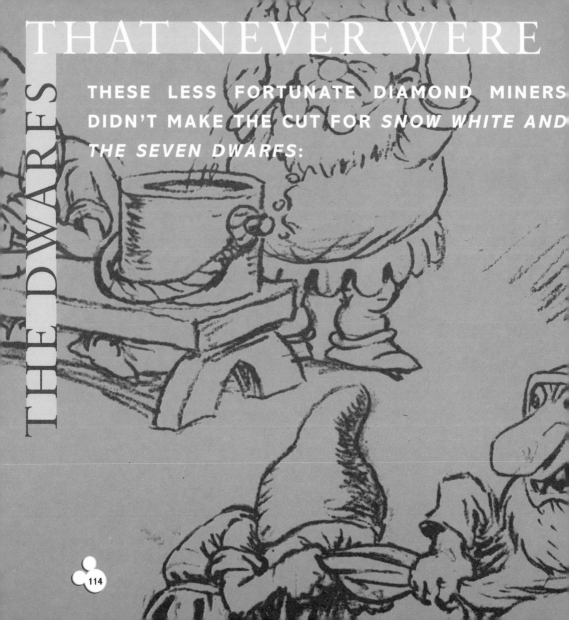

THAT NEVER WERE

THE DWARFS

THESE LESS FORTUNATE DIAMOND MINERS DIDN'T MAKE THE CUT FOR *SNOW WHITE AND THE SEVEN DWARFS*:

Awful • Baldy • Blick
Burpy • Deafy • Flabby
Flick • Frick • Gabby • Glick
Gloomy • Hoppy • Jumpy •
Lazy • Nifty • Puffy • Quee •
Shorty • Snick • Sniffy •
Stubby • Swift • Tubby •
Weepy • Wheezy • Whick

THE 1930S were tough years for sales. Although moderately successful with attempts to license Mickey Mouse toys and products, the Disney brothers weren't overly pleased with their merchandising agents. Then, in 1932, Herman "Kay" Kamen telephoned Walt with a proposition he couldn't refuse. "I don't know how much

HERMAN "KAY" KAMEN:
MERCHANDISE MAN

business you're doing," Kamen said, "but I guarantee you that much business and fifty percent of everything I do over that amount." Kamen got the job.

The master salesman single-handedly revolutionized Disney's merchandising, making deals with only the most reputable companies, ensuring the strictest quality control and accuracy of character likeness. Kamen not only racked up the profits for the Disney Company, but also pumped lifeblood into businesses hit hard during the Depression. Kamen sold the Ingersoll Watch Company on the idea of a Mickey Mouse watch, resulting in the single most popular Disney product of all time. The toy train manufacturer, Lionel Corporation, bounced back from bankruptcy with the sales of Minnie and Mickey windup handcars.

Kamen also published *Mickey Mouse Merchandise* catalogs, featuring hundreds of items from toothpaste to dishes, and the first *Mickey Mouse Magazine,* which was distributed by dairies, movie theaters, and department stores.

For the next seventeen years, Kamen continued working miracles, setting new standards for the Disney company that other businesses were wise to mimic. Tragically, in 1949, Kamen died in an airplane crash—the same year the 5-millionth Mickey Mouse watch was sold.

1. Be a man.

2. When life's a drag, cross-dress!

3. Need a change? Start with a haircut.

4. Practice spitting.

5. Be disruptive and unruly;
   if possible, start a fight.

6. Show fondness for your commanding
   officer by kicking his butt.

7. Think of a girl worth fighting
   for... even if it's yourself.

8. Never underestimate the power
   of a snow job.

9. If your dreams of becoming the
   perfect bride go up in flames,
   blame it on the match(maker).

10. For that extra dose of confidence,
    always keep a dragon in your pocket.

Walt Disney's Official

Davy Crockett LUNCH

with Fess Parker as Davy

DC-1
(Kit with bottle)

DC-B
(bottle separate

IF ANYONE AT THE DISNEY STUDIO could have predicted the national mania that broke out over a legendary American, the creators of *Davy Crockett* wouldn't have killed off their hero at the Alamo during the third show.

DAVY CROCKETT

Walt Disney's decision to produce *Davy Crockett* for the 1954–55 TV season came about almost by chance. Disney wanted a series he could link to Disneyland's Frontierland, and suggested Paul Bunyan or Johnny Appleseed. Once he heard the Davy Crockett idea, Disney gave producer Bill Walsh and writer Tom Blackburn the green light to draw up storyboards.

Three hour-long shows had Davy in hand-to-hand combat, raising Cain in Congress, and defending the Alamo. The only problem: each segment fell short by about five minutes. Disney asked George Bruns to compose "a little throwaway melody" for filler. In thirty minutes, Bruns tossed off the "Ballad of Davy Crockett," which wrangled the number-one slot on the Hit Parade for thirteen weeks, selling more than 7 million copies in its first six months. More than forty artists, including Burl Ives and Steve Allen, covered the song.

The Crockett craze fueled a merchandise frenzy. The demand for coonskin caps forced the wholesale price for skins to jump from 50¢ to $5 per dozen. Thousands of Crockett accessories lined toy shelves and clothes racks—from trading cards and lunch boxes to western wear and pj's. Scores of Crockett knockoffs flooded the marketplace after a Baltimore court ruled that "Davy Crockett" was in the public domain.

Disney extended the trilogy with two more prequels and two feature films. Three decades later, the studio tried to rekindle the Crockett flame with five more shows, but nothing could match the unprecedented popularity of Disney's first Davy.

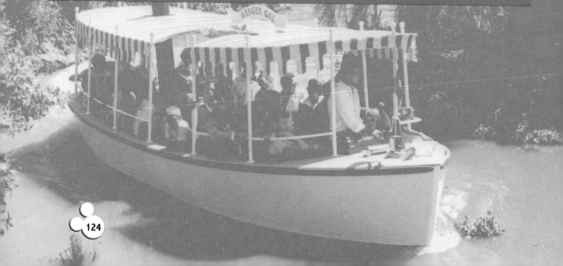

From the stagecoaches of the Old West to technological marvels of the future, Walt Disney spent his entire life fascinated with modes of travel, old and new. His theme-park vision incorporated numerous ways to transport visitors around without detracting from the scenery or polluting the environment. Whether by land, air, or water, there's always more than one way to journey:

* Americana comes to France aboard paddle-wheel *Mark Twain Riverboat,* cruising down the Rivers of the Far West.

* In Disneyland Paris, the steam train *Eureka* starts its morning journey. Each day trains carries thousands of guests on tracks that circle Disney parks.

* Walt Disney World Tomorrowland Transit Authority operates on environmentally sound linear-induction motors.

* FriendShip water taxis ferry passengers to different locales along World Showcase Lagoon at Epcot.

* Horse-drawn carriages, horse-drawn trolleys, jitneys, and a motorized fire engine offer one-way trips down Main Street.

* At Walt Disney World, the *Liberty Belle Riverboat* moves along Rivers of America on an underwater rail.

* The Jolly Trolley weaves its way through Mickey's Toontown offering passengers a rocking-and-rolling one-way trip.

* Monorail trains glide around the Disney parks in California and Florida; the first such trains to operate in the United States.

* A double-decker omnibus, electric car, and surrey have all transported guests up and down Main Street at Disneyland.

* At Disneyland, adventurers can float back in time on the *SS Columbia.* The craft is an exact replica of the 1787 *Columbia Redivivia,* the first American vessel to circumnavigate the globe.

BRITISH-BORN ROBERT STEVENSON became enchanted with the silver screen while a science student at Cambridge in the mid-1920s. While working on his thesis, the twenty-two-year-old Stevenson saw his first motion picture, *Sally, Irene, and Mary* (1925), starring a young Joan Crawford.

It changed his life. He forgot all about the paper and pursued a career in filmmaking. By 1932, he had directed *Happy Ever After* (a.k.a. *A Blonde Dream*), the first of nearly fifty films.

In 1939, Stevenson captured the attention of David O. Selznick—the same producer responsible for luring Alfred Hitchcock to the United States. Although Stevenson came to the United States and remained under contract with Selznick for ten years, he never directed for him. Stevenson would go on to make films for Howard Hughes at RKO as well as direct popular television programs such as *Alfred Hitchcock Presents* (1955) and *Gunsmoke* (1955–1956).

Stevenson's big break came in 1956 when he signed on with Walt Disney for *Johnny Tremain* (1957). Thereafter, he directed numerous live-action classics: fantasy (*Darby O'Gill and the Little People*, 1959), drama (*Old Yeller*, 1957), slapstick-satire (*The Absent-Minded Professor*, 1961, and *The*

Love Bug, 1969), and musical-fantasy extravaganzas (*Bedknobs and Broomsticks*, 1971, and *Mary Poppins*, 1964).

Stevenson elicited sterling performances from Julie Andrews, Sean Connery, Angela Lansbury, and Peter Ustinov, as well as Disney favorites Annette Funicello, Tommy Kirk, and Hayley Mills. "I don't direct actors too much," he explained. "I provide the atmosphere and mood in which they can do their best." His directorial formula paid off. By 1977, Stevenson's nineteen Disney films had raked in $750 million. That year *Variety*, the show-biz bible, hailed Stevenson as "the most commercially successful director in the history of films."

	MALEFICENT	GENIE
MISSION	Curse fulfillment	Wish fulfillment
CREDENTIALS	Mistress of All Evil	Bona Fide, Certified Genie of the Lamp
TEMPERAMENT	Malevolent	Benevolent
LEISURE ACTIVITY	Zapping imbecilic goons and performing nefarious machinations	Cracking imbecilic jokes and performing notorious impersonations
WEAPONRY	All the powers of Hell at her fingertips	Phenomenal cosmic powers up his sleeve
ACCESSORY	Horned hood	Goofy hat
ACCOMMODATIONS	A stone throne on Forbidden Mountain	An itty-bitty lamp in the Cave of Wonders
PREFERRED TRANSPORTATION	Flying ball of gaseous light	Flying carpet
PREFERRED TRANSFORMATION	Wicked, fire-breathing dragon	Witty, show-stealing gagger
WORDS OF ADVICE	"Stand back, you fools!"	"You fool, be yourself!"

133

IN

THE WAl

THIS CER

This Certifies that

S

is the record holder of

FULL-PAID AND NON-ASSE

The Walt Disney Company

© 1986 The Walt Disney Company

...ER THE LAWS OF THE STATE OF CALIFORNIA

...ISNEY COMPANY

...SFERABLE IN THE CITY OF BURBANK OR NEW YORK

...IMEN

...ARES WITHOUT PAR VALUE OF THE COMMON STOCK OF

...able on the share register of the Corporation by the holder

ONE OF WALT DISNEY'S more unlikely friendships was that with the surrealist artist Salvador Dali. Their mutual appreci-

SALVADOR DALI

ation led them to collaborate on a film. When the press mocked their efforts, Disney scoffed, saying "The thing I resent most is people who try to keep me in well-worn grooves."

In the mid-1940s, Salvador Dali came to Hollywood to work on Alfred Hitchcock's thriller *Spellbound*. In January 1946, Disney hired Dali to work on the short *Destino*. Dali created numerous sketches for the film, which was to incorporate live-action dance sequences with surrealistic animation scenes. He conceived of telephones with daddy-longlegs limbs, newspapers with scorpion legs, and a ballerina with a baseball head. Dali admitted he knew nothing about baseball, but as an artist, the game obsessed him; he said it represented "*le regard de l'univers*" (the gaze of the universe). Dali's vision, however, went over Disney's head and failed to meet the expectations of both artists. After the completion of an eighteen-second test for the film with a $70,000 price tag, the two mutually agreed to abandon the project.

Dali's short-lived influence at the studio had a lasting effect on some of Disney's subsequent films, as evidenced in the surrealism of *Alice in Wonderland*, which was in production during Dali's tenure, as well as the *Bumble Boogie* sequence of *Melody Time*, a musical fantasy of a bee's nightmare.

Dali and Disney remained lifelong friends, and spoke of working together on future projects. In the 1950s, Disney visited Dali at his home in Spain, where they discussed creating films based on *The Adventures of Don Quixote* and *El Cid*.

CALARTS

By THE 1930s, Walt Disney's aspirations in animation extended far beyond the conventions of the day. Wanting to train an entirely new breed of animation artist, he arranged for employees to attend classes at The Chouinard Art Institute. When the studio faced difficult times and could no longer afford the classes, school founder Nelbert M. Chouinard waived the fees. Disney never forgot that generosity; he returned the favor with donations during the school's troubled times in the 1950s.

Disney soon learned that Chouinard would need more than money to keep the school going. It needed modernization. He commissioned a research firm to conduct a study and recommend solutions. During the course of this research, Disney learned that another California art school, the Los Angeles Conservatory of Music, had also fallen into serious economic hardship. By 1960 a plan had gelled. The two schools would combine to form a new establishment, offering degrees in the visual and performing arts. Disney envisioned a place where students could learn every facet of the arts, and where established artists such as Salvador Dali and Pablo Picasso could give guest lectures. The following year, the California Institute of the Arts, known as CalArts, opened its doors to students.

NOTEWORTHY ALUMNI

Kathy Baker, actress
John Baldessari, visual artist
Bruce Berman, producer-film executive
Jamie Bishton, dancer
Ross Bleckner, visual artist
Chris Buck, director
Tim Burton, director-producer
Gary Chang, film composer-musician
Brenda Chapman, director
Sean Daniel, producer-film executive
Eric Fischl, painter
Jill Geigerich, visual artist
Guillermo Gomez-Peña, performance
    artist-playwright
Ed Harris, actor
David Hasslehof, actor-producer-singer
Bill Irwin, actor-playwright-new vaudevillian
Chuck Jones, animator
Glen Keane, animator
Mike Kelly, visual artist
Robert Glenn Ketchum,
    environmental photographer-author
Suzanne Lacy, visual artist
James Lapine, playwright-director
John Lasseter, animator-director
Kevin Lima, director
Loretta Livingston, dancer
Rob Minkoff, director
Thom Mount, producer-film executive
John Musker, director
Lari Pittman, visual artist
Michael Pressman, producer-film executive
Paula Rasmussen, opera singer
Paul Reubens, actor-writer-producer
Ed Ruscha, visual artist
David Salle, visual artist
C. Henry Selick, film director
Carl Stone, composer
Gary Trousdale, director
Carrie Mae Weems, visual artist-photographer
Kimball Wheeler, singer
Nedra Wheeler, jazz musician
Kirk Wise, director

139

Top View

BEFORE THE CREATION of Disneyland, Walt Disney and his artists were hard at work formulating a new kind of animation: Audio-Animatronics. Disney put artist Ken Anderson in charge of developing the very first prototype for the new medium, a 3-D dancing man. The actor Buddy Ebsen agreed to model for the part, and danced on film so that artists and technicians could study every movement.

Anderson's design called for a miniature stage built on top of a series of hand-cut metal cams that prompted the dancer's movements. Walt Disney himself did most of the construction for the dancing man display,

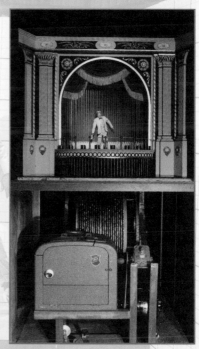

THE DANCING MAN

including attempting to carve the 9-inch Ebsen look-alike—but he quickly gave up and relied on the talents of a sculptor. Disney employed a movie projector to turn the cams, as well as provide the sound track synchronized to the dancing man's movements.

Although the dancing man never had a public audience, the very first Audio-Animatronics figure paved the way for the development of a revolutionary technology that would eventually become a hallmark feature of many of Disney's theme-park attractions.

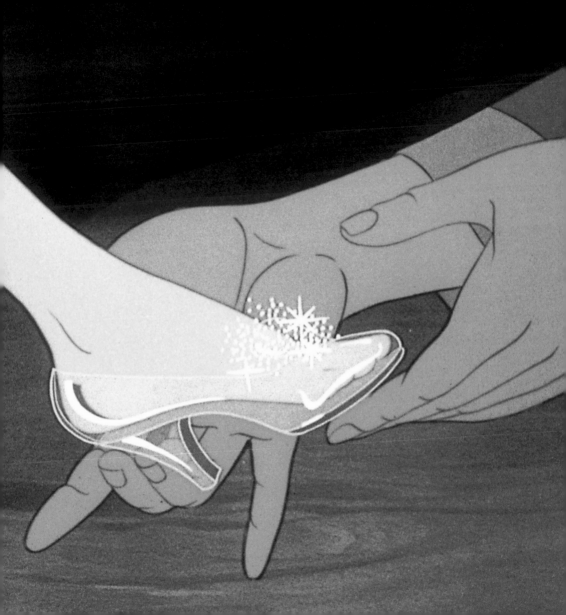

DID CINDERELLA WIN her Prince Charming because her feet were dainty? According to Charles Perrault, French author of the original fairy tale more than 300 years ago, Cinderella did not have exceptionally small feet. Her slipper was merely a story device to help the Prince track down the elusive beauty from the Royal Ball. Her famous slipper wasn't even originally made of glass. A mistranslation into English rendered *pantouffle en vair* (fur slipper) into *en verre* (glass).

In 1950, the year of *Cinderella*'s release, the Disney Studio anticipated questions about the actual shoe size of the animated cinder girl and distributed several press releases discussing the future princess's pedal extremities. Initial facts and figures of the eighteen-year-old blue-eyed blond starlet depict her as 5' 4", 120 lbs., with a shoe size "in proportion to her stature." To drive the point home further, the studio divulged shoe sizes of other contemporary movie stars: Shirley Temple (4A), Bette Davis (4½),

IF THE SHOE FITS...

Ginger Rogers (5½), Rita Hayworth (6), Ann Miller (7½), and "curvaceous" Lucille Ball (8), with a size "not out of keeping with her figure."

The question of Cinderella's shoe size is best answered by Disney animator Ward Kimball, who, when asked about it, aptly replied, "Why the *right* size, of course!"

Mr. Stork (*Dumbo*, 1941): "... Dear Jumbo Jr., happy birthday to ... you!"

Flower as an adult (*Bambi*, 1942): "*Twitterpated?*"

Cheshire Cat (*Alice in Wonderland*, 1951): "Most everyone's mad here ... you may have noticed that I'm not all there, myself."

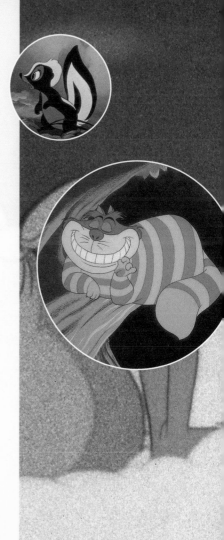

Amos (*Ben and Me*, 1953): "Joke!? You call this a joke!?"

Kaa (*The Jungle Book*, 1967): "Trust in me...."

Winnie the Pooh (*Winnie the Pooh and the Honey Tree*, 1966; *Winnie the Pooh and the Blustery Day*, 1968; *Winnie the Pooh and Tigger, Too!*, 1974; *Many Adventures of Winnie the Pooh*, 1977): "I'm so rumbly in my tumbly— time for something sweet...."

Roquefort (*The Aristocats*, 1970): "Did somebody say 'cheese'?"

Did you know? Sterling Holloway gave life to Woodsey the Owl, who appeared on television in the 1970s and 1980s with his famous words to the wise: "Give a Hoot! Don't Pollute!" He also played Sugar Bear (from the Post Sugar Crisp commercials) in the 1964 TV series "Linus the Lionhearted."

WORLD WAR II took a toll on Disney's earnings: 45 percent of the company's income that had been coming from foreign markets totally dried up. The studio desperately needed to find a project that would provide substantial profits at a production cost that wouldn't break the bank.

Dumbo took less than eighteen months to complete. The final cut ran sixty-four minutes, ten minutes shy of a normal feature film. Disney's distributor, RKO, demanded that the film to be longer, but Disney claimed he'd already stretched the story farther than he'd

DUMBO: CHEAPER, FASTER, BETTER

One day, Walt Disney came across a simple story he thought he could make cheaply: an illustrated tale by Helen Aberson and Harold Perl that recounted the trials and travails of a flying elephant. Disney bought the rights and in three minutes' time outlined the plan for *Dumbo*.

Economy was the key to making *Dumbo*. Supervising director Ben Sharpsteen discarded drawings that could hamper production and kept expenses down to a trim $800,000—a modest sum compared to *Fantasia*'s $2.28-million or *Pinocchio*'s $2.6-million budgets.

intended. Besides, ten more minutes would cost the studio $500,000—money it didn't have to spend.

Released in theaters in October 1941, *Dumbo* ultimately earned $2.6 million. *New York Times* critic Bosley Crowther called it Disney's "most winsome" film, "the one that leaves you with the warmest glow." *Dumbo* also prompted Algonquin Round Table regular Alexander Woollcott to write Disney a personal letter of thanks, lauding the film "as the highest achievement yet reached in the Seven Arts." He confessed: "During the Christmas holidays, I did nothing but sleep, dine with Frank Sullivan, listen to Churchill, and go to see *Dumbo* [three times]. That's what I call a good life."

WORLD WAR II essentially turned the Disney studio into a military zone. Virtually overnight, 93 percent of the studio's output was under government contract to benefit the war effort. Disney produced scores of military training, educational, and propaganda films for the United States and Canada, as well as created cartoons highlighting

the importance of paying income tax, salvaging kitchen grease to create glycerin, and recycling rubber.

Requests for military insignia flooded the studio. Enthusiasm for the designs was so great that Walt Disney needed to assign a special unit of artists who could devote all of their time toward meeting the demands. By the end of the war, studio artists had created no less than

DISNEY'S DOGTAG DAYS

1,200 insignia, featuring major and minor Disney characters. The insignia appeared on U.S. aircraft, submarines, badges, posters, stamps, pins, and match-books. But the designs weren't limited to the U.S.—orders poured in from France, Poland, Britain, South Africa, and even the American Volunteer Group of the Chinese Air Force.

DISNEY QUEST

Billed as an indoor interactive theme park, DisneyQuest takes the fun to new—and virtual—dimensions. For a generation of thrill seekers who have been weaned on the Internet, the idea of sitting back, relaxing, and enjoying the ride doesn't offer the same level of wonder as it once did. Adventure lovers can both be in the driver's seat and make up the ride as they go along.

Launched in June 1998, the five-floor DisneyQuest melds hands-on technology with futuristic attractions. More than 250 rides and games ranging from simple to supercharged can be experienced solo or with a group. With locations in Orlando, Chicago, Philadelphia, and Baltimore, DisneyQuest fare includes:

* CyberSpace Mountain, a design-it-yourself virtual roller coaster. Players link 10,000 feet of track, incorporating dips, loops, rolls, and twists, then test their own ride in hydraulic pitch-and-roll motion simulators.

* Pirates of the Caribbean: Battle for Buccaneer Gold, a 3-D group swashbuckler. A party of four boards a pirate-ship motion platform and battles Jolly Roger and his ghost ship to defend the gold.

* Ride the Comix, a laser battle with super villains in a 3-D comic-book setting.

* Virtual Jungle Cruise, where travelers paddle turbulent rapids down a digital river into a primeval world.

* Invasion, a 360° alien landscape where a pilot and three gunners need to rescue stranded colonists.

* Mighty Ducks Pinball Slam, in which players are transformed into human joysticks.

* Buzz Lightyear's AstroBlaster, a bumper-car-esque experience that lets riders target each other with asteroid cannons.

WHENEVER THE CREATIVE SPARK inspired Walt Disney to try something new, he generally turned to his brother Roy to handle the financing. But often, when Roy said "No," Walt heard "Go." In December 1952, when Walt didn't get what he wanted from his brother, he set up his own company to finance and plan Disneyland. He called it WED Enterprises (after his initials).

Walt pulled together some of his key artists, engineers, and designers to do something never before attempted: design and develop a theme park that would make guests feel as if they were part of a film. The WED team crafted Disneyland from concept sketches, architectural models, special-effects developments, and pure imagination. Walt wanted nothing to inhibit or limit their innovations... not even the sky.

In 1986, WED became Walt Disney Imagineering (WDI), and the forces behind it, Imagineers. Now more than a thousand Imagineers strong, WDI has grown from one small studio without heat or air-conditioning to more than two dozen buildings on a hundred acres of Disney property. A unique amalgam of architects, machinists, technicians, carpenters, custodians, and other creative professionals, they provide the wizardry behind Disney's multidimensional worlds. From conception to completion, Imagineers have put every Disney theme park on the map, as well as the resorts,

IMAGINEERS: DISNEY'S WIZARDS

After Disneyland opened, Walt wanted WED to continually "plus" the park, allowing its evolution to be as creative as the team of people behind it. Thereafter, WED remained a core entity behind Disney development.

cruise ships, office buildings, landscapes, and architectural marvels outside the parks. Not one stone is left unturned—even wallpaper and trash cans are designed to themed perfection.

BLACK SUNDAY

Disneyland's grand opening on July 17, 1955, went down in history as a day riddled with chaos and bad press. Walt Disney later dubbed it Black Sunday.

* Counterfeiters quintupled the number of invitation-only grand-opening tickets, flooding the park with as many as 27,000 more guests than anticipated.

* A local strike created delays in laying asphalt on park grounds. The freshly laid material plagued high-heeled women, whose spikes sunk deep into Main Street.

* A plumbing strike forced Disney to choose between working toilets or drinking fountains. He opted for toilets. Even so, the lines for the restrooms snaked around the buildings.

* The heat of the day mounted, causing water-fountain-seeking patrons to buy up refreshments. Park restaurants quickly ran out of all food and drink.

* A reported gas leak in Tomorrowland caused the fire chief to rope off the area, closing it completely.

* Someone sabotaged Fantasyland, cutting electrical cables and stranding people in the rides' gondolas and cars.

* Water flooded the deck of the Mark Twain Riverboat when too many passengers ran to the same side.

* During the dedication ceremony, actor Bob Cummings got caught kissing a dancer in Frontierland, and the emcee mistakenly introduced Davy Crockett actor Fess Parker as Cinderella.

* The critical press predicted failure for the theme park, citing lack of alcoholic beverages as one of the major flaws.

* Opening day aired before a live television audience, complete with bloopers, miscues, and on-screen goofs.

Yet, in spite of the snafus, Disneyland opened its gates again on Monday to a stream of visitors. Within seven weeks, 1 million people came.

TIMON & PUMBAA'S

1. Put your behind in your past.

2. When the world turns its back on you, turn your back on the world.

3. Keep a lion around—you never know when he might come in handy.

4. Don't let your friends stand downwind (especially if you're a warthog).

5. When you're hungry, you can always rustle up some grub... er, grubs, under a log. (They're slimy, but surprisingly satisfying.)

6. If you're a pig, eat like one.

7. When trying to outsmart hyenas, dressing in drag and doing the hula can be very effective.

8. Always maintain a carefree outlook: no worries. But in the face of danger, scream.

9. Stick with your friends to the end.

10. Remember: home is where your rump rests. (We recommend a nice rock that overlooks the savanna....)

IN THE SPRING OF 1941, the United States hadn't yet entered the war, but was actively involved in preventing Fascist encroachment across its borders. President Franklin D. Roosevelt had particular concerns about South America, which had for decades attracted many Italian and German immigrants. As a way to quash increasing Axis sentiment south of the border, the president established the Good Neighbor Policy, a plan that called for U.S. dignitaries to visit South American countries and strengthen hemispheric solidarity.

John Hay Whitney, director of the motion-picture division for Nelson Rockefeller, Coordinator of Inter-American Affairs (CIAA), thought it would be a good idea to enlist Walt Disney for a goodwill tour. Mickey Mouse and Donald Duck were immeasurably popular characters in South America. So, why not send someone whose work the South Americans already knew and admired?

Disney agreed, and in August boarded a DC-3 with his wife and a carefully chosen group of fifteen animators, story developers, and designers. For the next three months, the so-called El Gruppo traveled through the Amazon, Rio de Janeiro, Buenos Aires, Chile, Lake Titicaca, and along numerous South and Central American coastal towns. Their duty was twofold: to engage in cultural exchange and to make a film.

The mission proved successful on both fronts. Everywhere they traveled, children and adults alike came in droves to see the Disney artists. The Latin music, dance,

GOODWILL TOUR

flavors, and customs inspired them as nothing had before. Their palettes exploded with color and vibrancy that reflected the spirit of all they had encountered as seen in the resulting films, *Saludos Amigos* (1943) and *The Three Caballeros* (1945).

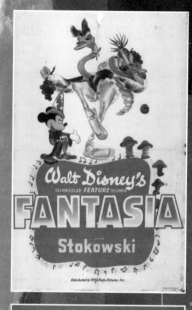

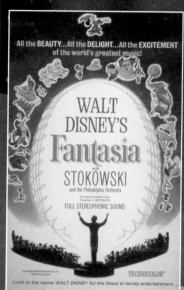

MICKEY
MOUSE
INGERSOLL

THE MICKEY MOUSE WATCH

IN NOVEMBER 1928, when Mickey Mouse made his debut on the American screen, the event marked both the best of times and the worst of times: the cheerful mouse danced his way into the hearts of people across the nation, promising a hopeful future for Walt Disney Productions. But in less than a year's time, the Great Depression changed the face of that future.

Not long after Walt was forced to sell his car in order to make his company's payroll, he met one of the greatest salesmen of his day, Kay Kamen. Kamen had the idea of putting Mickey on the face of a watch and approached the Ingersoll watch company about making it happen. The watches hit the market in June 1933, and by December, more than 900,000 had been sold. The Mickey Mouse watch boomed and became one of the single most sought-after items in 1933—and the trend only grew. At the 1933 World's Fair in Chicago, the Mickey Mouse watch outsold the Fair's own commemorative watch three to one.

The Mickey Mouse watch did more than save Walt Disney Enterprises from hard times, it saved Ingersoll from bankruptcy. By 1935, increased sales forced Ingersoll to multiply its work force 14 times—from 200 to 2,800 employees. The watch face that launched a thousand Mickeys made for not-so-depressing times during the Depression.

Mickey Mouse

Miekie	Afrikaans
Mickey	Arabic
Mai Kay Shiu Shu	Cantonese
Mickey Mouse	Danish
Mikki Hiiri	Finnish
Micky Maus	German
Mikki Maous	Greek
Miki Eger	Hungarian
Topolino	Italian
Mickey Mouse	Japanese
Michael Musculus	Latin
Mi Lao Shu	Mandarin
Mikke Mus	Norwegian
Mickey	Portuguese
Mikki Maus	Russian
El Ratón Mickey	Spanish (South America)
Musse Pigg	Swedish
Miki	Turkish
Mic-Kay	Vietnamese

Donald Duck

Donald	Afrikaans
Batu	Arabic
Anders And	Danish
Aku Ankka	Finnish
Donald Duck	German
Andrés Önd	Icelandic
Donal Bebek	Indonesian
Paperino	Italian
Donaldus Anas	Latin
Donald Duck	Norwegian
Pato Donald	Portuguese
Pato Donald	Spanish (South America)
Kalle Anka	Swedish

دونالد دك

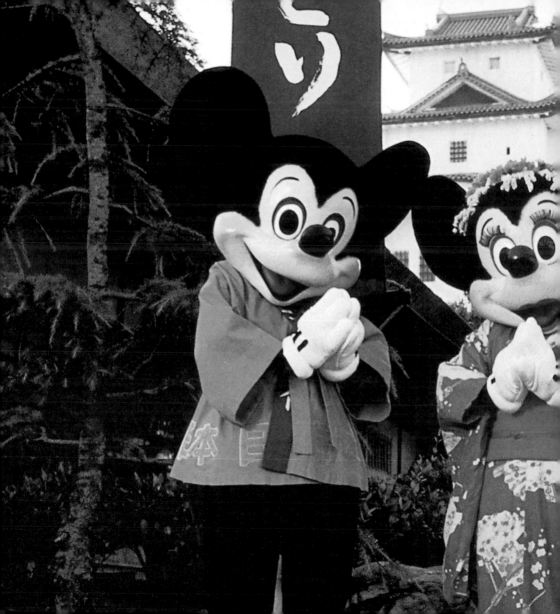

THE HALL OF PRESIDENTS in Liberty Square at Walt Disney World started as the brainchild of Walt Disney, who wanted to create an exhibit for Disneyland that would dramatize American history. To prepare the attraction, Disney designers researched hairstyles, jewelry, fabrics, and tailoring

HAIL TO THE CHIEFS

techniques from each president's time period. Culling information from diaries, paintings, and government archives, Disney artists attempted to authenticate every detail, down to the cushions on George Washington's eighteenth-century chair and the braces on Franklin D. Roosevelt's legs. The installation of the Great Seal, located in the Hall's rotunda, needed congressional approval. Only two others exist: at the White House in Washington, D.C.,

and at the Liberty Bell, in Philadelphia, Pennsylvania.

All the presidential figures move and gesture, and some even appear to whisper, but until the addition of Bill Clinton in 1993, only Mr. Lincoln spoke. Character actor Royal Dano, who bears a resemblance to the sixteenth president, recorded Lincoln's voice. President Clinton was the

first leader to record his own voice from the White House. President George W. Bush will do the same. The only other celebrity voice is that of poet Maya Angelou, who narrates the show.

The lifelike Audio-Animatronics figures need continual maintenance. All presidents have at least one change of clothing... and personal beauticians. Each night, makeup artists freshen up the presidential faces for their next appearance.

Dis
A

$1.00

EST. PRICE 91c
FED. TAX 9c

TOT

neyland

ULT   2

ADMIT ONE

000001

IN 1996, LOTTERY WINNERS TOOK up residence in a newly constructed southeastern town. The jackpot: Not the daily double. Not $2.5 million. But a draw toward a lifestyle that claimed to have it all: Rockwellian Americana wired for the future. Which is exactly what the founders of Celebration, Florida, had in mind.

OUR TOWN: THE NEXT GENERATION

Inspired by Walt Disney's vision of a community of the future, Disney executives in the mid-1980s made plans to develop land adjacent to Walt Disney World. In visceral response to strip-mall sprawl and car culture, planners worked in the spirit of New Urbanism, a philosophy that integrates mixed housing with interconnected streets in a town with a distinct center and edge. Beyond the realm of planned communities, Celebration would include a viable downtown retail district, a state-of-the-art hospital, progressive kindergarten through twelfth grade education, and a community intranet with high-speed data access offering every residence voice, data, and video network communications designed to facilitate a sense of community.

Working with internationally renowned architects, including Robert A.M. Stern, Robert Venturi, Denise Scott Brown, Michael Graves, and Aldo Rossi, developers built a new town from the ground up, melding a pre-1940s architectural style with twenty-first-century amenities. Residential districts emulate Classical, Victorian, Coastal, Mediterranean, French, and Colonial Revival styles. Miles of nature trails and walking paths loop through town, along with a par-72 golf course, village recreation areas, and a lake in the heart of downtown.

The result: an evolving community with a layout and infrastructure that facilitates interaction and a sense of civic commitment.

WANTS TO BE A CAT

WHY EVERYBODY

* Domesticated humans fall head over heels for you.

* Life is full of artistic opportunities— after all, your mews is forever with you.

* You can always join the chorus with the Tin Pan Alley cats.

* Despite life's challenges, you always land on your feet.

* You can tear the house down with the scat cats.

* Everything you do is simply *purrfect*.

* You've elevated the catnap to an art form.

* You're merely a lick away from a perfect coiffeur—*et voilà* ...glamour puss!

* The whole world is your scratching post.

* Why avoid trouble? You've got nine lives.

DISNEYLAND

SCHEMATIC AERIAL VIEW
APPROX. 45 ACRES
WITHIN RAILROAD TRACKS

EVER SINCE THE Sunday afternoons when Walt Disney would take his young daughters to amusement parks, he became obsessed with building a better place where parents and children could have fun together.

It took more than fifteen years for Walt to formulate his plans, which expanded from two and a half acres to 270 acres. As Walt's vision grew, so did the proposed price tag—from $1.5 million to $17 million. Walt and his brother Roy did everything they could to raise money, but they still needed more, so Roy planned a trip to New York to sell the idea to investment bankers.

Saturday morning, September 26, 1953, two days before Roy's trip, Walt called up artist Herb Ryman, asking him how quickly they could meet. Ryman gave him the choice of fifteen minutes "as is," or thirty minutes, bathed, shaved, and dressed. Fifteen minutes later, Walt greeted Ryman at the studio and launched into his plans for Disneyland and drawings that they needed to show to New York bankers. "I'd love to see what you're going to do," said Ryman. "Where is it?" Walt replied, "You're going to do it!"

THE LOST WEEKEND

Ryman objected, concerned that he couldn't pull off something so grand in a weekend and that results would be disastrous and embarrassing for both of them. Walt offered to stay with him all weekend and they struck a deal. For the rest of what came to be known as the lost weekend, Walt described the park while Ryman drew. Monday morning, Roy flew to New York with a drawing of Disneyland in his hands.

The plan worked. Roy came back to California with the money, and plans for Disneyland were kicked into high gear.

CONVENTION

On May 14, 1972, Sotheby's held a unique auction featuring items of Disney memorabilia, launching a Disneyana tradition at many major auction houses. Disneyana's continuing popularity gave rise to collectors' gatherings, and by 1992, The Walt Disney Company took notice and hosted the first Official Disneyana Convention at Walt Disney World. Since then the annual event has attracted thousands of enthusiasts for collectibles, seminars, and socials. Among the fare:

* specially created limited-edition, signed convention art

* antiques and collectibles shows offering independent collectors' wares dating back to the 1920s

* the Official Disneyana Convention Auction promising one-of-a-kind items

* an artist's showcase where artists and sculptors meet and greet guests

* hands-on interactive workshops

* dignitary speakers discuss subjects from animation to collectibles

* gala receptions, banquets, and entertainment

DISNEYANA THEMES

* "Mickey" September 24-27, 1992

* "Bandleader Mickey" September 1993

* "Sorcerer Mickey" September 1994

* "Neat & Pretty" September 1995

* "The Brave Little Tailor," September 1996

* "Villains," September 1997

* "75 Years of Love and Laughter," September 1998

* "Safari Adventure," September 1999

* "It's a Small World," September 2000

* "A Disney Family Reunion," September 2001

Walt Disney's

Song of the South

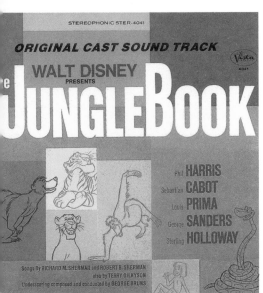

STEREOPHONIC STER-4041

ORIGINAL CAST SOUND TRACK

Vista
4041

WALT DISNEY
PRESENTS

e JungleBook

Phil **HARRIS**
Sebastian **CABOT**
Louis **PRIMA**
George **SANDERS**
Sterling **HOLLOWAY**

Songs By RICHARD M. SHERMAN and ROBERT B. SHERMAN
also by TERRY GILKYSON
Underscoring composed and conducted by GEORGE BRUNS

Disneyland
RECORD
HIGH FIDELITY
DQ1289

STEREO

WALT DISNEY presents

IT'S A SMALL WORLD

18 FAVORITE FOLK SONGS

DISNEYLAND BOYS CHOIR
UNDER DIRECTION OF PAUL SALAMUNOVICH
ARRANGEMENTS BY WILLARD JONES / PRODUCED BY CAMARATA

Disneyland
ST 3966

WALT DISNEY'S
THE ENCHANTED TIKI ROOM
FROM DISNEYLAND
THE ORIGINAL SOUND TRACK OF THE TIKI ROOM AND THE ADVENTUROUS JUNGLE CRUISE

A MAGNIFICENT FULL-COLOR ILLUSTRATED BOOK AND LONG-PLAYING RECORD
Copyright Walt Disney Productions

MM22   33⅓ RPM

OFFICIAL MICKEY MOUSE CLUB

WALT DISNEY presents

Holidays with
the **Mouseketeers**

A SONG FOR EVERY HOLIDAY

			2	3		5
7	8	9	10	11	12
13		15	16		18	19
20			24		26
27					

NEW YEAR'S DAY
VALENTINE'S DAY
EASTER
FATHER'S DAY
MOTHER'S DAY

4th OF JULY
HALLOWEEN
THANKSGIVING
CHRISTMAS
and others.

WHEN THE TIME CAME to bring Louie the orangutan to life for *The Jungle Book* (1967), Disney turned to Dixieland Jazz scat cat Louis Prima. Renowned for his wild numbers in Las Vegas and Lake Tahoe, Prima provided the winning combination of rhythm and style for the jive-talking jungle king's speaking and sing voice. The pinnacle of King Louie's performance comes during the pied-piper parade, "I Wanna Be Like You." The animated sequence features Baloo the bear-cum-ape and King Louis dancing to the song's infectious jazz rhythm, followed by the pal-frond bearing Flunkey Monkey and Mowgli. When composers Richard and Robert Sherman first shared the concept with Prima, he exclaimed, "What do you want to do? Make a monkey out of me?"

They nodded.

"Ya got me!" he wailed.

KING LOUIE

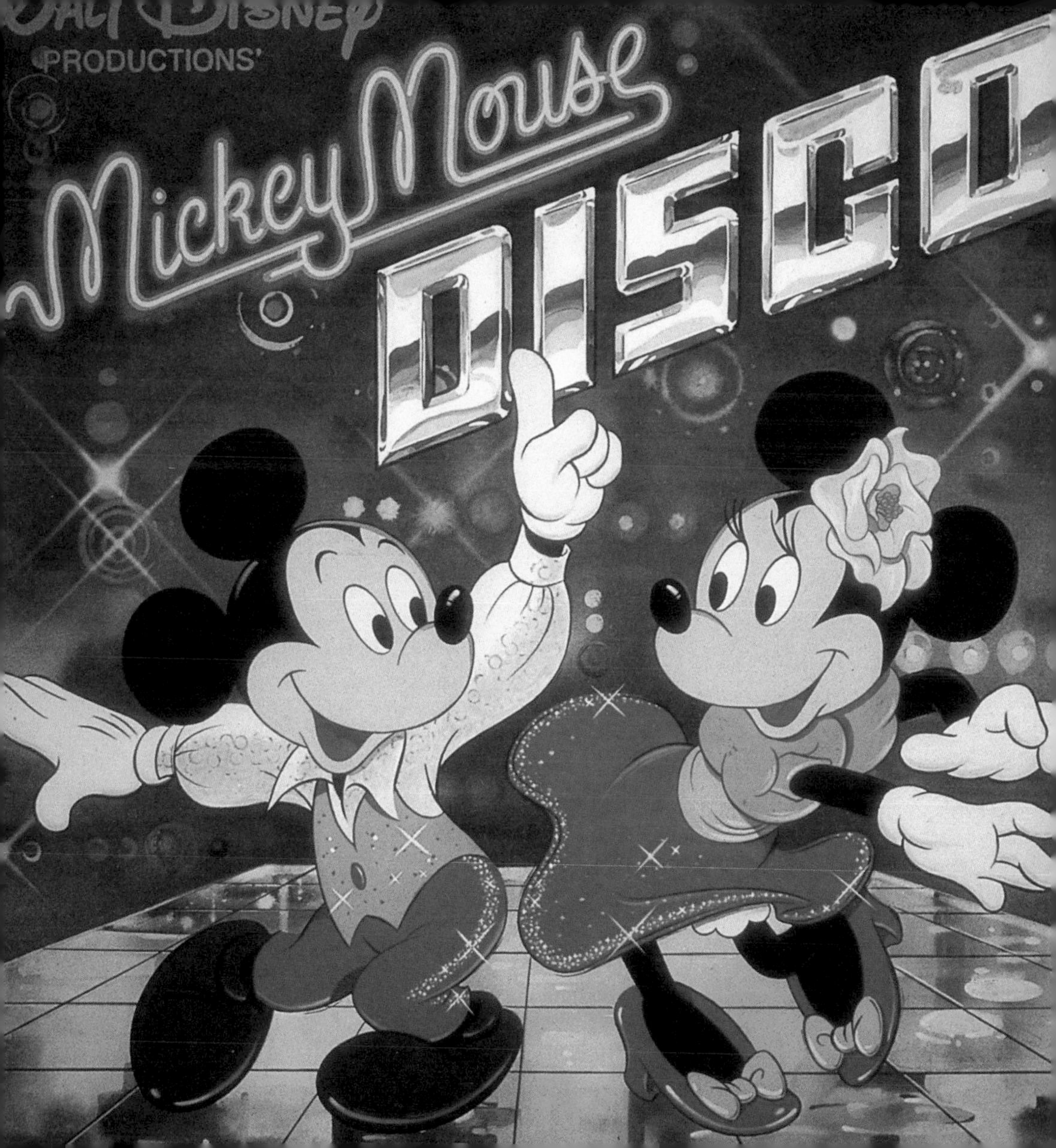
WALT DISNEY
PRODUCTIONS'
Mickey Mouse
DISCO

IN NOVEMBER 1978, *Life* magazine hailed disco as no mere fad, but rather as "a national fever sweeping the society we live in." Disco fever affected more than 37 million Americans who boogied down in no fewer than 10,000 new discotheques that had popped up across the nation. Disco music and disco-influenced songs dominated *Billboard* charts, raking in 4 billion dollars of revenue. Virtually no one escaped its influence.

Not even Mickey Mouse.

The Mouse celebrated his fiftieth birthday on the cover of *Life's* Disco issue. That month, he hobnobbed with dozens of Hollywood celebrities on the specially aired television show *Mickey's 50* and even got his own star on the Hollywood Walk of Fame.

Mickey embraced middle age decked out in *Saturday Night Fever* style. Gone were the familiar red shorts. Instead, he donned wide

DISCO MICKEY

© WALT DISNEY PRODUCTIONS

DISCO MICKEY

collars and bell-bottoms, perfectly flared over a tricolor illuminated dance floor, as displayed on the Disco Mickey wristwatch, issued in 1979. At ten minutes before four o'clock, Mickey strikes John Travolta's quintessential disco pose.

JOE GRANT: MODEL ARTIST

WALT DISNEY FIRST DISCOVERED Joe Grant in 1933 through his celebrity illustrations in the *Los Angeles Record*. Disney hired Grant to work on *Mickey's Gala Premiere,* which is chock-full of classic Grant Hollywood caricatures, including Greta Garbo, Clark Gable, Mae West, Douglas Fairbanks, and Marlene Dietrich. Thereafter, Grant stayed on board in the story department, where he quickly won Disney's respect and trust. He worked on numerous shorts in the '30s and became one of the key character designers for the 1937 feature, *Snow White and the Seven Dwarfs.* Grant's work on that film's character model sheets inspired Disney to create the Character Model Department. And Disney handpicked Grant to run it.

Grant quickly brought together a cracker-jack team of artists who devoted themselves to model sheets of character sketches and ideas for future projects. No model sheet was acceptable without his stamp of approval: "OK, J.G." And Grant was picky; his sensibility greatly influenced the look of Disney films during the company's Golden Era. Grant's department soon expanded to create 3-D sculptures, models, and props for characters as well. In time, the department also became the source for live-action costumes and makeup.

Grant left the Studio in 1949 to pursue his own endeavors for thirty-eight years before rejoining Disney Feature Animation to work on films from *Beauty and the Beast* to *Fantasia/2000.* His significant contributions to Disney films earned him the Disney Legend award in 1992.

IN THE HEART of New Orleans Square at Disneyland, nestled behind nineteenth-century French Quarter balconies and ironwork, is the lesser-known members-only Club 33. Walt Disney made plans for the private restaurant, adjacent to his personal apartment, where he and his family could entertain guests and VIPs with fine food in an elegant atmosphere away from the day-to-day hustle and bustle of the park. Disney and his wife, Lillian, traveled extensively to New Orleans in search of period antiques to enhance the private eatery's décor. Plans for the restaurant included original concept art for New Orleans Square, as well as a host of Audio-Animatronics birds equipped with speakers and microphones for interactive live entertainment with diners on special occasions. The club would also be a place for Disney to store hunting trophies he had received as gifts.

Disney never had the opportunity to dine there; the restaurant officially opened in May 1967, five months after his death. Planners decided to turn it into a private club where people could become members for a fee—ranging from $5,000 to $20,000. Named for its address, 33 Royal Street, the restaurant is the

CLUB 33

only place in the park that serves alcohol. The club is reminiscent of Prohibition-era speakeasies; guests can enter only after ringing a hidden doorbell and requesting admittance through an intercom.

A second Club 33 opened in Disneyland Tokyo in 1983. Located above the World Bazaar shops, Tokyo's version is considerably larger, with more rooms, a larger dining area, lounge, and bar. It offers an ideal view of the castle and the finest food in the park.

TONY'S FAMOUS

For the perfect romantic evening, try this classic dish, heavy on the "meat-sa-balls"...

SAUCE

- 2 tbs. olive oil
- 1 small onion, minced
- 2 cloves garlic, minced
- 2 1/2 cups chopped tomatoes
  (with juices)
- 4 tbs. fresh basil, chopped
- 1/4 tsp. dried oregano, crumbled
- 1/4 tsp. sugar
- salt and pepper, to taste

MEATBALLS

- 1 lb. ground beef
- 1/2 cup bread crumbs
- 1 large egg
- 1 clove garlic, minced
- 1/4 cup finely chopped onion
- 2 tbs. minced parsley
- 2 tbs. fresh chopped basil
- 1/4 tsp. ground nutmeg
- 1/2 tsp. salt
- 1/4 tsp. ground black pepper
- 1/2 cup grated Parmesan cheese

- 2 tbs. pine nuts
- 2 tbs. olive oil

- 1 pound spaghetti, freshly cooked

FOR SAUCE: Heat oil in heavy saucepan. Add onion and garlic; sauté about 5 minutes. Add tomatoes, basil, oregano, sugar, and bring to a boil. Reduce heat; simmer until sauce thickens, about 1 hour. Season with salt and pepper.

FOR MEATBALLS: Combine beef, bread crumbs, egg, garlic, onion, parsley, basil, nutmeg, salt, pepper, Parmesan, and pine nuts. Mix thoroughly. Shape into 1 1/4-inch balls. Heat oil in heavy saucepan. Add meatballs in batches and cook until brown on all sides, about 8 minutes. Drain off the fat.

Combine meatballs with sauce and serve over spaghetti.

ONE EVENING IN 1934, Walt Disney invited a group of animators to join him on a sound-stage lit by a single bulb. There, he outlined the story of *Snow White and the Seven Dwarfs*.

Disney's plan broke new ground in many ways: the film would not be a gag-driven short, but a full-length animated

DISNEY'S FOLLY

feature; it would call for a more natural environment than any previous cartoon; and it would include creatures that Disney's animators had yet to master—humans.

Production costs mounted, fueling doubts inside the company as well as throughout the film industry. Critics dubbed it "Disney's Folly," predicting that the project would be the demise of the Disney studio. At a time when cartoon shorts cost $30,000, Disney projected *Snow White* would cost half a million to produce. But unlike the shorts, for which Disney's distributor paid upon delivery, as Roy Disney once recalled, "If we had flopped with *Snow White*, we were gonna flop with our own money."

More than 750 artists—including 32 animators, 102 assistant animators, 107 in-betweeners, 66 inkers, and 178 painters—worked around the clock to create no fewer than 250,000 drawings and cels. *Snow White* became the largest collaborative art project in the country. The budget soared to an unprecedented $1,488,000.

Snow White and the Seven Dwarfs premiered at Los Angeles' Carthay Circle Theatre on December 21, 1937, to a host of Hollywood illuminati. Clark Gable and Carole Lombard were among those wiping their eyes at the film's conclusion.

Disney's gamble paid off in spades. *Snow White* earned $8.5 million worldwide, at a time when the price of admission was twenty-three cents for an adult and ten cents for a child.

UNITED
STATES

6c

IN THE MID-1940S, during the Disney Studio's production of wartime educational and military training films, Walt Disney became entranced by the stories of H. T. Kavanagh. Disney's enduring interest in folklore coupled with his Irish heritage made the idea of a film about leprechauns seem like an ideal pursuit.

After the war's end, Disney sent artists to Ireland to research material for the story. True to the *London Observer*'s remarks about grown men traveling thousands of miles in search of mythical beings, by 1948, Disney went to Eire himself and publicly announced plans for the production of *The Little People*, the film's original title.

LUCK OF THE IRISH

After nearly two decades of research and development, *Darby O'Gill and the Little People* premiered in Dublin, Ireland, on June 24, 1959. The numerous special effects are truly convincing, even by modern standards. Yet the film performed poorly at the box office. Disney surmised that American moviegoers had difficulty understanding the actors' brogue, and reissued a dubbed version. Nevertheless, the film's many strengths proved to be a boon for some. Leading actress Janet Munro starred in the subsequent films *Swiss Family Robinson* and *Third Man on the Mountain*. The little-known actor Sean Connery went on to play Wronski in a television version of *Anna Karenina* and later made frequent appearances as an undercover Brit, starting with *Dr. No* in 1962. *Darby O'Gill* proved to be a major catalyst for the success of director Robert Stevenson, who became one of Hollywood's most prolific directors in the following decades.

TINKER BELL'S RÉSUMÉ

MISS TINKER BELL
HANGMAN'S TREE, NEVER LAND
SECOND STAR TO THE RIGHT

OBJECTIVE:

High-placed position in youth-oriented entertainment market

PROFESSIONAL EXPERIENCE:

Youth Group Tour Leader: Conducted atmospheric trips from London to Never Land; provided knowledge of local lore of Never Land attractions, including Pirate's Cove, Mermaid Lagoon, Skull Rock, and Hangman's Tree

Captain, Lost Boys Militia: Assembled and led squad in sortie against incoming hostile aircraft; responsible for troop morale

Actress: Starring role in major motion picture, numerous television appearances, and theater productions

Television Personality: Introduced weekly children's variety show and television specials

Special Effects Producer: Rendered pixie dust effect, flying sequences, and special light displays in film, television, video, and multimedia markets

Theme Park Pyro-Technician: Responsible for the igniting of nightly fireworks display at major theme parks around the world

SPECIAL SKILLS:

Levitation; cartography; glowing; fluent in French, Japanese, English, and Pixie; high-speed flight; escape artist

EDUCATION:

Bachelorette of Fairy Magic, The Marc Davis Academy of Prestidigitation; Magna cum Illuminata

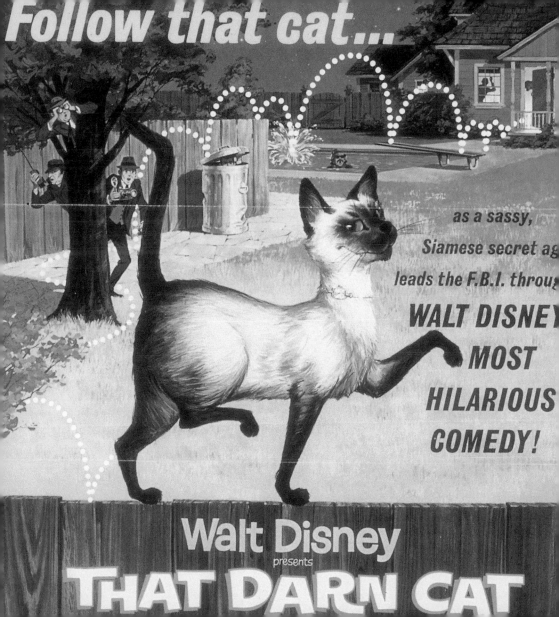

THAT DARN CAT made the incredible journey from the pound to the pictures, thanks to Disney's chief animal trainer Bill Koehler, who rescued the Siamese cat Syn from a southern California Humane Association pound. Sheila Burnford, author of the book *The Incredible Journey*, personally hand-picked Syn from the audition lineup of more than 100 hopeful cats to star in the 1963 movie of the same title.

According to Koehler, Syn was so comfortable acting in the wilderness for *The Incredible Journey* that it took some time for him to adapt to the indoor movie sets for the filming of *That Darn Cat* (1965). Fortunately, ample preproduction time allowed Syn to become familiar with his primary costar, Hayley Mills. Koehler recalled that during the long rehearsals, "she held and carried Syn in her arms and cradled him in her lap while sitting.

Within a few days, there was no interrupting his purring when he was handed to Hayley!"

Times critic Bosley Crowther hailed Syn as the film's "coolest,

SYN most controlled, intelligent, and indeed believable participant." All that work, acclaim, record box-office grosses—and yet, no Oscar. But the American Humane Association came to the rescue by honoring Syn with a Patsy Award for Best Animal Performer in 1966.

ASSEMBLING THE BEAST

ONE OF THE MOST COMPLEX creatures ever to appear in a Disney animated film is the enchanted prince-cum-beast in *Beauty and the Beast*. Neither villain nor hero, but an amalgam of both, the Beast is a tragic figure bound by animal and human characteristics.

Animator Glen Keane faced the challenge of creating the complex being. Keane had drawn beastly characters in previous Disney films, including the bears in *The Fox and the Hound* and Ratigan in *The Great Mouse Detective*. But for the Beast, Keane drew his inspiration from a host of critters... at the Los Angeles Zoo. There, he spent hours sketching buffalos, gorillas, wolves, bears, and mandrills. At

one point, producer Don Hahn recalled that Keane got so inspired, "he even asked to get into the cage with the gorilla so he could feel what it was like to be in the presence of such a powerful primate." The zookeeper, however, kept Keane from losing his head and denied his request.

Keane's ultimate assemblage of the Beast incorporated traits from several animals. The creature had a bear's body supported by a wolf's hind legs and tail. His head became a composition of a mandrill's face with a gorilla's brow, a buffalo's beard, a boar's tusks and nose, and the mane of a lion. Keane considers the Beast's transformation into a prince to be among the best animated scenes of his career "because that was so much an expression of my own art and what I felt spiritually is important in my life: a transformation from the inside out.... [B]y animating that, I really felt that I was expressing everything about myself."

For TV viewers who grew up watching The Wonderful World of Disney, some of the most beloved shows were the live-action adventures starring animals. From The Ballad of Hector, the Stowaway Dog to Twister, Bull from the Sky, these animal stars all managed to overcome trials and tribulations with flair:

Brimstone, The Amish Horse
Carlo, The Sierra Coyote
Charlie, The Lonesome Cougar
Chester, Yesterday's Horse
Chico, The Misunderstood Coyote
Cristobalito, The Calypso Colt
Deacon, The High Noon Dog
Flash, The Teenage Otter
Greta, The Misfit Greyhound
Nikki, Wild Dog of the North
Nosey, The Sweetest Skunk of the West
Pancho, The Fastest Paw in the West
Ringo, The Refugee Racoon
Salty, The Hijacked Harbor Seal
Sammy, The Way-Out Seal
Sancho, The Homing Steer
Shokee, The Everglades Panther
Solomon, The Sea Turtle
Stub, The Best Cow Dog in the West

SAMMY, THE WAY-OUT SEAL, ET AL.

SAMMY

A KANSAS CITY MAN of Frisian descent, Ub Iwerks dropped out of high school and became one of the most gifted animators of the twentieth century. He met Walt Disney at his first job, and within a year the two nineteen-year-olds formed their own short-lived studio, the first of several joint endeavors. By 1924, Disney had established himself in Hollywood, and Iwerks joined him as his chief animator.

When Disney lost the rights to Oswald the Lucky Rabbit in 1928, he also lost his core artists. Iwerks alone remained loyal. This act proved to be the single most critical event in the history of the Disney legacy. Disney and Iwerks created a new character based on the

UB IWERKS: UBER ANIMATOR

swashbuckler Douglas Fairbanks and Charlie Chaplin's Tramp who would become one of the world's most recognizable icons—Mickey

Mouse. At the impossible rate of 700 drawings per day, Iwerks single-handedly animated the first Mickey Mouse cartoon, *Plane Crazy*, in two weeks.

After the 1940s, Iwerks put the Disney Studio at the cutting edge of special photographic effects by making breakthroughs in optical printing; combining live action and animation in *Song of the South* (1946); modifying a Xerox machine to transfer animators' drawings directly to celluloids as

first used extensively for *101 Dalmatians* (1961); and developing the traveling-matte system used in *Mary Poppins* (1964). His innovations extended to the Disney parks, with Circlevision 360 and special effects for It's a Small World, Pirates of the Caribbean, and the Hall of Presidents, his last project.

The first googly-eyed Mickey as seen in *Plane Crazy* (1928) went barefoot and gloveless.

In the early thirties, Mickey appeared with solid oblong pupils and sported his signature gloves and bulbous shoes.

By 1940, the whites of Mickey's eyes are clearly defined as seen in his first feature film, *Fantasia*, in which he stars as the Sorcerer's Apprentice.

Mickey sports a dapper, refined look in *The Nifty Nineties* (1941). His snout has slightly lengthened, his cheeks have become more pinchable, and his ears are less than perfectly round.

In the "Mickey and the Beanstalk" segment of *Fun and Fancy Free* (1947), our hero has lost some of his lankiness from the early years. His modified upturned nose hints at his spunky character.

By the 1950s, Mickey's larger eyes are a testament to his baby-face appeal to a younger audience.

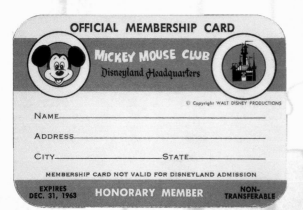

OFFICIAL MEMBERSHIP CARD

MICKEY MOUSE CLUB
Disneyland Headquarters

© Copyright WALT DISNEY PRODUCTIONS

NAME

ADDRESS

CITY   STATE

MEMBERSHIP CARD NOT VALID FOR DISNEYLAND ADMISSION

EXPIRES
DEC. 31, 1963   **HONORARY MEMBER**   NON-
TRANSFERABLE

Within the first month *The Mickey Mouse Club* was a smash hit, second only to the special telecast of the 1955 World Series in ratings. Fan mail piled up daily, Mouseketeer wanna-bes purchased 24,000 mouse-ear hats per day, and millions of preteens recited their favorite stars at roll call time: Sharon, Cubby, Bobby, Lonnie, Tommy, Annette, Darlene, Karen, Doreen....

The Mickey Mouse Club featured animated segments, Donald Duck's infamous gong, *The Mickey Mouse Club Newsreel*, Jiminy Cricket's educational segments, a puppet named Sooty, serialized adventure stories, and the Mouseketeers' daily themes:

MICKEY MOUSE CLUB DAILY

BABY BOOMERS ACROSS AMERICA—in fact, three-quarters of the nation's viewing population—planted themselves in front of television sets every weekday at five o'clock sharp, ready to chant the familiar theme song, "M-I-C...K-E-Y...M-O-U-S-E!"

MONDAY: Fun With Music Day

TUESDAY: Guest Star Day

WEDNESDAY: Anything Can Happen Day

THURSDAY: Circus Day

FRIDAY: Talent Roundup Day

DUCKBURG'S WEALTHIEST RESIDENT, Scrooge McDuck, makes no bones about how he got so rich. He credits all three cubic acres of money to the very first dime he earned shining shoes at age ten.

"Old Number One," as Scrooge fondly coined his first tenpenny piece, has been the source of his luck. According to the annals of Duckburg, the dime dates back to 1875. Two years later the Number One Dime found itself in the possession of Howard Rockerduck (father of John D. Rockerduck) who crossed the Atlantic en route to Glasgow. Something of a

And so it did.

Of all the millions Scrooge has amassed since then, he has never forgotten the dime that started it all. He has jealously guarded Old Number One, keeping it framed on the wall or prominently displayed under a glass case. But for safety's sake, Scrooge

SCROOGE'S OLD NUMBER ONE

playduck, H. Rockerduck wanted to impress the Scottish lasses by tossing his pocket money to children. Scrooge's sisters Hortense and Matilda happened to be among the crowd and scooped up Rockerduck's change. The sisters placed it in the care of their father, who in turn thought it would make the ideal incentive to inspire Scrooge to earn money.

keeps the Number One Dime locked securely away in his money bin, far away from the evil duck Magica de Spell. Her *raison d'être* has been to melt Scrooge's coin into an amulet that she believes will make her the richest duck in the world. Whether because of Scrooge's masterful ability to hoard his money or de Spell's knack for foibles, Old Number One remains, for the time being, the good luck charm of Scrooge McDuck.

```
medieval ancestor Andold
Temerary, a.k.a. Wild Duck
```
```
Cornelius Coot
(founder of Duckburg)
```
```
Grandma Elvira Coot          Grandpa Humperdink Duck
```
```
Daphne     Goostave        Eider Duck     Lulubelle       Quackmore      Hortense
Duck       Gander                         Loon
```
```
           Gladstone       Abner          Fethry        Dumbella       Donald
           Gander          "Whitewater"   Duck          Duck           Fauntleroy
                           Duck                                        Duck
```
```
                    Huey           Dewey          Louie
```

THE DUCK FAMILY TREE

DISCLAIMER: Due to Donald's inability to keep his ducks in order, some of the family tree facts may be scrambled.

*** Great grand niece and nephews of Elvira Coot**

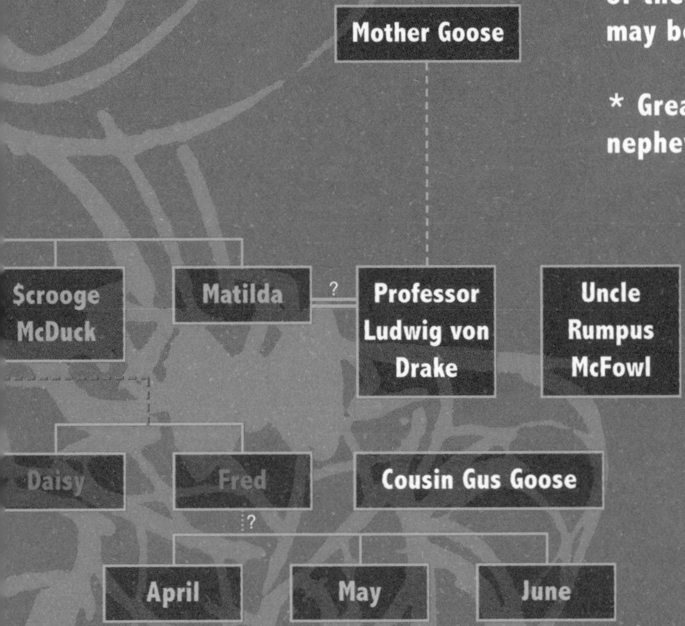
Mother Goose
$crooge McDuck
Matilda
?
Professor Ludwig von Drake
Uncle Rumpus McFowl
Daisy
Fred
Cousin Gus Goose
?
April
May
June

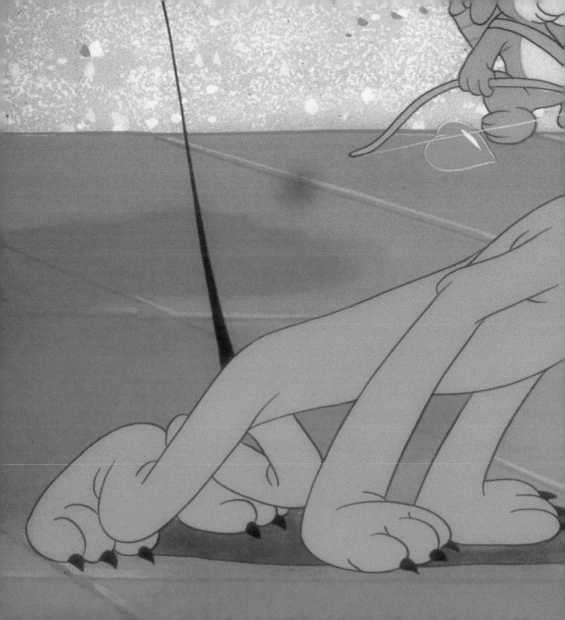

WHEN WALT DISNEY reviewed the nearly completed story for a film based on Rudyard Kipling's *Jungle Book*, he decided to scrap everything…with one exception: Baloo. Unlike some of the film's other character designs, the original design for Baloo by Disney Legend Ken Anderson remained true to form in the film's final version. The studio's recreation of the Kipling story had remained faithful to the text, resulting in a dark score with stern characters. Disney wanted a complete rewrite of the musical score, keeping only Baloo's song, "Bear Necessities," written by Terry Gilkyson.

Meanwhile, animators had been testing styles and voices for the small part of Baloo the bear when

"I wasn't so good at reading to my two daughters when they were little." After reading for Baloo's part, Harris knew he couldn't play a bear. But when animators asked Harris to act the part *his* way, suddenly Baloo came to life. Harris's performance loosened and livened up the character to such a degree that it demanded a role much bigger than a cameo. Harris's own toe-tapping rhythm and improvised lines, such as "I'm gonna knock your roof off," gave animators the perfect inspiration to create the jungle bum, Baloo.

Released on October 18, 1967, *The Jungle Book* turned out to be the last animated feature that Walt Disney

BALOO, THE NECESSARY BEAR

Disney suggested the popular '40s bandleader and radio, TV, and film personality Phil Harris for the part. Harris was as surprised as the animators at the suggestion. "I don't do voices," he admitted.

supervised. His complete overhaul of the film bore little resemblance to Kipling's original story, which, for Disney turned out to be well worthwhile: the film earned $13 million at the box office. Its success, largely thanks to Baloo's "just playin' it cool," led the studio to begin its first formal recruiting program for animation artists.

DISNEY'S WONDERFUL WORLD OF TELEVISION

PETER PAN'S FAVORITE pixie, Tinker Bell, ignited the fireworks every Sunday night at 7:30 on *The Wonderful World of Disney*. The program aired on NBC from September 14, 1969 to September 2, 1979. Beloved for its animal stories (*Lefty, The Dingaling Linx*; *Inky the Crow*), dramatic mini-series (*The Scarecrow of Romney Marsh, The High Flying Spy*), cartoon shorts (*It's Tough to Be a Bird, The Adventures of Chip 'n Dale*), and theatrical releases (*The Shaggy Dog, The Computer Wore Tennis Shoes*), the show soared in popularity, ranking several times in Nielsen's "Top 10" television series.

WINNIE THE POOH started his life as the stuffed bear of a young English boy, Christopher Robin Milne. The name "Winnie" was likely inspired by Christopher's favorite black bear in the London Zoo, a mascot of the Canadian Army named for the city of Winnipeg. As for Winnie's surname, Christopher had another stuffed animal he dubbed "Pooh," and the name stuck with Winnie as well.

In the 1920s, when his son was a toddler, A. A. Milne wrote a collection of stories titled *Winnie-the-Pooh* about the world of the Hundred-Acre Wood, where Christopher Robin and his toy animal friends had adventures. Illustrated by E. H. Shepard, these stories gained popularity in England and the United States, and were eventually translated into more than three dozen languages.

Nearly forty years after their initial publication, Walt Disney obtained film rights to the stories and transformed the well-loved bear into Technicolor. The 1966 featurette *Winnie the Pooh and the Honey Tree* proved to be a challenge for the animators, who tried to preserve the spirit of the 2-D black-and-white line drawings, while adding color and 3-D movement. But American audiences welcomed the film, prompting three additional featurettes. The first of which, *Winnie the Pooh and the Blustery Day*, won the 1968 Academy Award for Cartoon Short Subject.

WINNIE THE POOH

Pooh lives on in educational films, television series, and merchandise—and into the twenty-first century. The Hundred-Acre Wood came to life at Tokyo Disneyland Fantasyland attraction, Pooh's Hunny Hunt (2000).

Did you know? Winnie the Pooh was essentially a bare bear until the 1940s, when F.A.O. Schwarz, the New York toy store, sold plush Poohs in shrunken T-shirts. By the time Pooh made his film debut, his red T-shirt had become a permanent fixture.

HAND PUPPETS

Of nine "Sleeping Beauty" characters.

Retail Price $1.00 each

PRINCE PHILLIP RING

With removable Sword of Truth.

Retail Price, 10c

M SHIMMEL SONS
16 West 19th St., New York 11, N. Y.

DOLL

3-Dimensiona
acter dolls an
plastic sheets.

ALDON
200 Fifth Ave

SCHOOL BAG

Of Vinyl coated Texon with detachable shoulder strap.

n a Dream.
98
MPANY
sburg, Wis.

Retail Price: $2.00
Service for two — 12 pieces (Not illustrated.)
Retail Price: $1.00
WORCESTER TOY CO.
93 Northboro St., Worcester 4, Mass.

DISNEYLAND PIN-UPS

"Sleeping Beauty" characters now join the famous Disney Pin-Up parade.

Retail Price: $2.49
THE DOLLY TOY Co.
Tipp City, Ohio

OUTS

Beauty" char-
on washable,
il Price: 49c
ES, Inc.
ork 10, N. Y.

CRIB MOBILE

Baby's first plaything...
"Sleeping Beauty" characters of washable plastic gently circle over baby's crib.

Retail Price: $2.00

ROCKETS TO THE MOON, people in space, laser beams: in the 1950s, such was fodder for fantasy, fiction, film—and scientists. Inspired by Jules Verne as a child, German-born Wernher von Braun devoted his adult life to making science fiction into fact. After his pioneering work on the V-2 rocket, which caused massive destruction in England and Belgium during WWII, he emigrated to the United States to develop spacecraft for the U.S. military.

Beginning in 1952, von Braun published his visionary rocket-ship designs in *Collier's* magazine, capturing the imaginations of about 4 million readers, including Disney producer Ward Kimball. The timing was perfect. Kimball needed to develop television concepts to promote Tomorrowland. He called von Braun, who jumped at the opportunity to work with Disney.

Von Braun served as technical advisor for *Man in Space* (March 1955), *Man and the Moon* (December

1955), and *Mars and Beyond* (Decembe 1957). With his academic-sounding Germa accent, von Braun's narration had a straight man charm that provided an amusing counter point to Disney's animation sequences. H envisioned reusable rockets gliding back t Earth, space suits allowing astronauts to wor in orbit, and space stations with complet living and working quarters. More than 4. million people tuned in to the first show prompting heightened public interest in spac exploration. Even one top Soviet spac official, Lenoid Sedov, tried to convince th president of the USSR's Aeronautica Federation to secure a cop of Disney's program to promote their space efforts.

Before long, Disney' "science factual" serie would no longer be glimpse of the future. By 1958, von Braun became director of NASA's George C. Marshall Space Center and developed the Saturn rockets, which put a man on the moo in 1969.

TO THE MOON:
WERNHER VON BRAUN

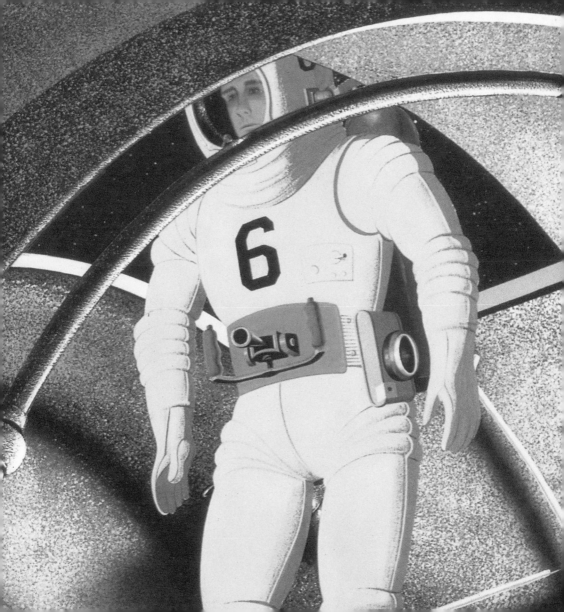

ATTRACTIONS

When considering the best possible place to build a new kind of amusement park, Walt Disney turned to the professionals at the Stanford Research Institute. Their pick: 160 acres in Anaheim covered with orange groves. Determined to see his plans through—and to the chagrin of his wife, Lilly, and brother, Roy—Disney borrowed heavily against his life-insurance policy, sold his vacation home, and plummeted into more than $100,000 of personal debt. But he managed to scrape enough money together to purchase the land and build Disneyland, a place, said Disney, "that will never be completed...as long as there is imagination left in the world."

After more than twenty years of planning, Disneyland opened its doors to a curious and eager public on July 17, 1955. By day's end, more than 28,000 people had experienced these attractions:

Autopia • Canal Boats of the World • Circarama • Fire Wagon • Golden Horseshoe Revue • Horse-drawn Streetcars • Jungle Cruise • King Arthur Carrousel • Mad Tea Party • Main Street Cinema • Mark Twain Steamboat • Mr. Toad's Wild Ride • Mule Pack • Penny Arcade • Peter Pan Flight • Santa Fe and Disneyland Railroad • Snow White's Adventures • Space Station X-1 • Surreys

THE XVIITH OLYMPIAD

In the early 1950s, New York socialite Alec Cushing approached the International Olympic Committee (I.O.C.) to consider his bid for the 1960 Winter Olympics. At the time, his Squaw Valley, California, resort had one ski lift and two rope tows.

Cushing, a master promoter, enlisted support from the California legislature, international delegates, and Walt Disney. With much ado, Squaw Valley beat out Innsbruck, Austria, and St. Moritz, Switzerland; the Lake Tahoe hamlet would host the games.

The I.O.C. built ski runs, ice-skating rinks, dormitories, water and sewage plants, and media facilities at a cost of nearly $9 million. Meanwhile, Pageantry Committee Chairman Disney spearheaded the games' ceremonies. He orchestrated the elaborate passing of the Olympic torch, to be jetted from Olympia to Los Angeles, site of the 1932 games, and carried by 600 high-school athletes to Squaw Valley. There, the 1952 gold medallist ski champion, Andrea Mead Lawrence, would carry it down the slopes to American speed skating champion Ken Henry, who would ultimately light the flame for the opening ceremony. A 2,000-member choir and 1,000-member orchestra would perform the Olympic hymn.

Disney artist John Hench set the stage. He designed the massive Tower of Nations, flanked by 24-foot-tall snow sculptures of a male and female athlete, and surrounded by thirty flagpoles representing the competing countries. In all, thirty giant snow sculptures adorned the scenery.

Just before the event, disaster struck. A thirty-hour torrential rainstorm turned the powdery slopes into rivers. Then, temperatures dropped, transforming the downpour into a 24-hour blizzard, putting snow back on the mountains, but threatening opening-day events. The snow continued to fall as the parade of nations began, but magically, the sun came out, and Disney's pageantry was hailed the finest of any Olympic Games to date.

salutes the athletes of the world

VIII OLYMPIC WINTER GAMES
CALIFORNIA 1960

DURING THE PAST three-quarters of a century, countless technological innovations

THE AGE-OLD STORYBOARD

have changed the way in which animated films are made. Celluloids have given way to computer generated images and painstaking manual tasks can now be done with the click of a mouse. One element, however, remains as vital to the process and as unchanged as the day it was introduced in 1931: the storyboard.

Disney scriptwriter Webb Smith first pinned sequential sketches on a four by eight foot fiberboard as a way to visualize a scene that before animators had only talked about. Suddenly, story developers could add, remove, or change the order of scenes with ease. In a single glance, the action, mood, and progression of the story would be evident without lengthy explanation or discussion. The storyboard instantly became an essential step in the entire filmmaking process, and soon became adopted industry-wide, for live-action and commercial production alike.

Storyboarding rarely starts from the beginning of a film. For *Mulan*, the first storyboard completed was sequence six in which Mulan determines to leave home—she takes her father's draft notice and sword, cuts her hair, and heads off to war. The simplicity of the sequence with its absence of dialogue establishes the film's visual and emotional power. The sequence became the core of the film, helping the filmmakers to find their main character.

6-46

6-47

CHIP AND DALE started their film career as trouble-making foes for Pluto and Donald Duck. Earlier films *Private Pluto* (1943) and *Squatter's Rights* (1946) depict both chipmunks with black noses. As their popularity increased, the chipmunks gained more distinctive characteristics, thanks to

CHIPMUNKS AHOY!

the developments of Jack Hannah. By their fourth film, *Three for Breakfast* (1948), the goofier Dale appears with a larger, reddish nose, a tuft of hair atop his head, and notable space between his two front teeth, whereas the practical-minded Chip tends to exhibit better leadership skills than his partner in crime. Chip and Dale starred in twenty-four shorts from 1943 to 1983.

WALT DISNEY FIRST DISCOVERED Donald Duck on the radio—as a comic doing a duck's rendition of "Mary Had a Little Lamb." Disney wanted his cartoon characters to have voices as fantastical as the animated drawings themselves. And Clarence "Ducky" Nash had that quality in spades.

Disney hired Nash to repeat his radio performance for the 1934 Mickey Mouse short *Orphan's Benefit*. Nash's portrayal of the hot-tempered, jibberish-squawking duck instantly won the hearts of Disney animators, and, ultimately, the duck stole the show from Mickey. Donald Duck's actual debut in the 1934 Silly Symphony *The Wise Little Hen* would be the first of more than 150 shorts and television shows voiced by Nash.

Since audiences hardly under stood Donald's explosive utterances, the animators took that into account. Either another character would repeat Donald's words, or the dialogue could be inferred through gags and pantomimes. The result: one of *the* most popular Disney characters of all time, starring in more films than Mickey Mouse himself.

Nash remained the voice of Donald Duck for fifty years—a longer run than Donald's classic pals. In 1983, director Burny Mattinson wanted to create a new short capturing the essence of Disney's golden era. *Mickey's Christmas Carol* starred the old favorites, including Mickey, who hadn't appeared in a short in thirty years. None of the original voice actors were available for recording—except Nash. When he came on the set, Mattinson recalls, "We looked at each other doubtfully as he adjusted his hearing aid. [When he spoke] his first words in character . . . a collective thrill went through the room. Everybody looked at each other and thought, Wow it's Donald Duck!"

CLARENCE "DUCKY" NASH

Long before an animated film is released, Disney's Animation Creative Services is on the front lines developing the advertising campaigns that establish the brand identity of the film. According to Fred Tió, Executive Vice President Worldwide Marketing, "the process is very collaborative, starting with discovering what makes each film unique and projecting what about the film will withstand the test of time." How do they do it? Here's a look at some past campaigns:

* Quirky newspaper ads featured title characters from *A Bug's Life* (1998): "Single Widowed Female" and "Bugs for Hire."

* With re-releases, such as *Fantasia* (1940) in the '50s, '60s, '70s, and '80s, new posters have been created to appeal to new generations.

* When the time came to create a poster for *Beauty and the Beast* (1991), the look of the Beast had not yet been fleshed out. But the problem proved to be a boon for the poster: dramatically silhouetted characters dancing in a shaft of light.

* The campaign for *Atlantis* (2001) relied on existing conceptions of the lost empire. Rather than reveal story lines from the film, the advertising materials play on the intriguing mythos surrounding Atlantis, tapping into the romance of adventure.

* The story of *Mulan* (1998) presented a unique challenge. Most Westerners knew nothing about the 2,000-year-old Chinese legend, nor how to pronounce it. The question was whether to go warm and fuzzy or adult. The solution was to present a dramatic poster that would honor the story as a legacy.

SUNKEN TREASURE retrieved from a world of silent
darkness that no man was meant to discover!

WALT DISNEY Productions' Robin Hood TECHNICOLOR® G

WALT DISNEY'S The Incredible Journey TECHNICOLOR®

SIZE OF CLARABELLE COW
IN COMPARISON
WITH MICKEY

THE HAND

THE HEAD
THE BELL →

← BE

SHE STARRED IN MORE THAN three dozen films, displaying her talent for music, dancing, singing, lovesickness, and gossip, yet Clarabelle Cow never enjoyed success in a leading role—she was destined to remain a member of the orchestra, the leading lady's companion, or simply an extra.

Clarabelle Cow, the large-nostriled, bucktoothed bovine started her movie career appearing as a nameless cow in the 1926 Alice Comedy *Alice on the Farm*, in which Julius the Cat makes repeatedly unsuccessful attempts to milk her. She debuted in the 1928 Mickey Mouse short *Plane Crazy*, but it wasn't until 1929 in *The Plow Boy* that she officially became known as Clarabelle.

In the 1930s, Clarabelle appeared in numerous Mickey Mouse shorts as well as Disney comic strips. She and her boyfriend, Horace Horsecollar, worked well together—their rubber-hose arms and legs were perfectly suited for dancing and performing countless physical gags rendered in the classic "squash-and-stretch" animation style.

Clarabelle also appeared on dozens of Disney merchandise products, including

CLARABELLE COW

toilet soap, tin tea sets, cookie boxes, and wristwatch boxes. Although her popularity peaked in the 1930s, her legacy continues. After cameo appearances in *Who Framed Roger Rabbit* (1988) and *The Prince and the Pauper* (1990), Clarabelle has reached a new generation of television viewers with several appearances in the 2000 season of Mickey MouseWorks cartoons.

E TICKETS

WHEN DISNEYLAND FIRST opened its doors to the public on July 17, 1955, an adult ticket cost $1 and served as general admission to all areas of the park. Three months later, the park offered ticket books with A, B, and C coupons good for specific rides and attractions throughout Disneyland. The following year saw a host of newcomers—Astro Jets, Tom Sawyer Island Rafts, and the Skyway to Tomorrowland and Fantasyland, as well as the new D ticket.

The E ticket entered the Disneyland ticket books in 1959, making its appearance the same year as the Matterhorn Bobsleds, the Monorail, the Submarine Voyage, and Fantasyland's Autopia. At 50¢ each, the coveted tickets admitted adventure-seekers to the most exciting attractions in the park, including Haunted Mansion, Pirates of the Caribbean, and ultimately, Space Mountain.

In 1982, Disneyland retired the E ticket along with the others in the Disneyland Ticket Book to usher in the Disneyland Passport. But the E ticket lived on in the local vernacular. In 1983, Sally Ride became the first American woman to go in space aboard the shuttle Challenger's STS-7 mission and described her experience as "a real E-ticket ride."

The E ticket continues to have a life beyond its initial 23-year run. Disneyland and Walt Disney World have created E-ticket after-hours events. A limited number of guests can, for a price, enjoy the parks' most popular attractions without the crowds. In winter 1986, the E ticket also resurfaced in the form of a magazine devoted to fans of Disneyland history.

NGS
o Disneyland Hotel & Return
VOYAGE

L WORLD
N BOBSLEDS

EAR JAMBOREE

ANSION
THE CARIBBEAN

TIKI ROOM
ISE

---

any other ''E'' attraction

E

COUPON

271

In 1959, Walt Disney had big plans to expand his four-year-old park. He wanted to open three new Disneyland attractions; his brother Roy preferred to wait a few years until they had financial solvency. But Walt went forward with his plans, knowing that his numbers man would figure out a

MATTERHORN

way to finance the projects. Walt told Joe Fowler, who supervised the construction of Disneyland, that he wanted to "make some snow and have a toboggan ride." Fowler discouraged the idea, citing problems with snow maintenance and water drainage.

So Walt got around the snow problem by building a mountain out of steel, wood, and plaster. Long inspired by family vacations to Europe, he modeled the exhibit after the Matterhorn Mountain in Switzerland. The 147-foot high structure is $1/100$ the size of its Swiss counterpart. Walt's toboggans became bobsleds, which travel on

cylindrical rails and urethane wheels—an innovative construction on which future roller coasters were modeled.

As Walt hoped, 1959 saw the opening of the Monorail, the Submarine Voyage, and the Matterhorn Bobsleds. Richard Nixon visited the park with his family to dedicate the opening of the Monorail. Nixon, along with Walt and his family, was one of the first to ride the Matterhorn Bobsleds. The Abominable Snowman didn't take up residence at the mountain until 1978.

In 1903, the New Amsterdam Theatre opened on New York's famed Forty-second Street, rivaling every other playhouse in the nation. The ornate marquee with its elaborate sculptures and strikingly modern art-nouveau design was but a mere taste of

Struggling and slipping into the red in 1929, the theater nonetheless ran popular shows including *The Band Wagon*, starring Fred and Adele Astaire.

THE NEW AMSTERDAM THEATRE:
THE HOUSE BEAUTIFUL

what theatergoers would find inside. The building, conceived by distinguished architects Henry Herts and Hugh Tallant, boasted two playhouses, an eleven-story office tower, seven floors of dressing rooms, unobstructed views from every seat in the acoustically perfect main theater, and a rooftop garden. The budget reflected the attention to detail—more than $1.5 million, double the cost of other theaters of the day.

The New Amsterdam's first decade saw lavish productions ranging from *Caesar and Cleopatra* to *Ben-Hur*. As host to the *Ziegfeld Follies* the New Amsterdam was at the center of American theater's Golden Era from 1913 to 1927.

By 1937, the New Amsterdam had gone the way of other Broadway theaters, and was converted into a movie house. Mismanagement and lack of upkeep took its toll on the theater in the late 1970s. By the early 1980s it fell into complete decay.

Not until the early 1990s, when New York began plans to revitalize the entire Forty-second Street district, would the New Amsterdam be reborn. Leased by The Walt Disney Company in 1995, and under the aegis of architect Hugh Hardy, a $36-million renovation got underway. Hundreds of specialists contributed to reinstating the theater's original glory while adding modern amenities. In 1997, the New Amsterdam's doors reopened to the public, beginning a new era of the House Beautiful.

DO: Keep a roaring fire in the hearth.

DON'T: Keep roaring at prisoners in the dungeon.

DO: Be your personal best.

DON'T: Be perfectly beastly.

DO: Shower your enchanted one with compliments.

DON'T: Drench the evening with complaints.

DO: Make a big ado over meals. Have music, fine silverware, suckling pig.

DON'T: Eat like a suckling pig.

DO: Show hospitality.

DON'T: Show hostility.

DO: Be generous.

DON'T: Forget that inviting someone to stay can get you into trouble.

DO: Be dashing and debonair.

DON'T: Pound down doors and make demands—that may not be the fastest way to one's heart.

DO: Keep a little candlelight glowing. It can add a spark of romance to any situation.

DON'T: Let a heated temper spark a conflagration.

DO: Initiate a date. A dinner invitation is always nice.

DON'T: Initiate a mandate. Threats of starvation can distract one from hunger for love.

DO: Give your love the freedom to leave.

DON'T: Let your love get away!

AND THE WINNER IS...

Since 1932, the Academy of Motion Picture Arts and Sciences has awarded Disney more than six dozen awards in nearly two dozen categories. Walt Disney personally won thirty-two Academy Awards, an amount that garnered him an entry in *The Guinness Book of World Records*. As of the turn of the century, the tally is:

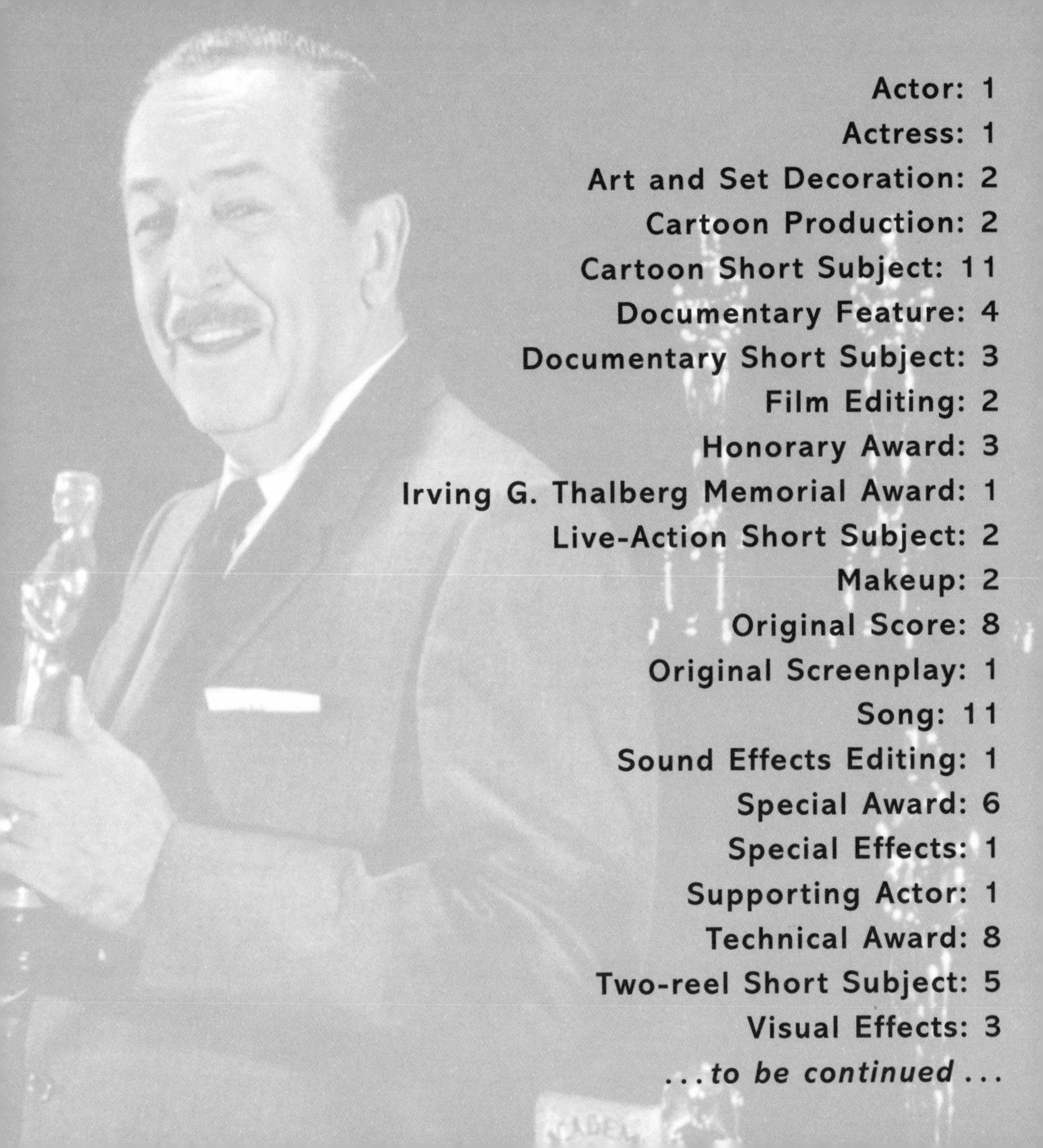

Actor: 1
Actress: 1
Art and Set Decoration: 2
Cartoon Production: 2
Cartoon Short Subject: 11
Documentary Feature: 4
Documentary Short Subject: 3
Film Editing: 2
Honorary Award: 3
Irving G. Thalberg Memorial Award: 1
Live-Action Short Subject: 2
Makeup: 2
Original Score: 8
Original Screenplay: 1
Song: 11
Sound Effects Editing: 1
Special Award: 6
Special Effects: 1
Supporting Actor: 1
Technical Award: 8
Two-reel Short Subject: 5
Visual Effects: 3

...to be continued ...

DISNEY CHALKED UP his thirty-sixth Silly Symphony with the 1933 Radio City Music Hall premiere of *Three Little Pigs*. At the time, he thought of it as an affable retelling of an old tale. Nothing prepared him for how thoroughly a Depression-weary audience would embrace the triumphant pigs and turn the film's lead song into a hard-times mantra.

HREE LITTLE PIGS

The public's overwhelming response forced the Disney brothers to scramble. Having never had a popular song before, they naturally didn't have any plans in place to publish sheet music or records. Theaters wanted to offer live orchestral accompaniment to Frank Churchill's "Who's Afraid of the Big Bad Wolf?" and Irving Berlin's music company requested the rights to publish the song.

In a fortuitous bit of timing, master of merchandising Kay Kamen had just signed an exclusive contract with Disney one month before the release of *Three Little Pigs*. Without missing a beat, Kamen launched in-store promotional campaigns, and soon the Big Bad Wolf and Three Little Pigs were appearing on wristwatches, clocks, board games, books, dolls, figurines, pencil boxes, and cardboard cutouts from cereal boxes.

The success of *Three Little Pigs* added up to $64,000 at the box office and prompted three Silly Symphony sequels, *The Big Bad Wolf* (1934), *Three Little Wolves* (1936), and *The Practical Pig* (1939). Although the Depression heroes enjoyed considerable popularity, none of the other films generated quite the sensation as did the first. About that, Disney wisely noted, "You can't top pigs with pigs."

d you know? Walt Disney's Three Little gs have supporting (live-action) roles Hal Roach's *Babes in Toyland* a.k.a. arch of the Wooden Soldiers (1934) arring Stan Laurel and Oliver Hardy.

When Disneyland opened its gates to the public for the first time, Disney invited the Mouseketeers to his apartment to witness the event. Mouseketeer Sharon Baird got a first hand glimpse of one man's dream come true: "He had his hands behind his back, a grin from ear to ear...a lump in his throat, and a tear streaming down his cheek."

The cozy apartment included a sitting room with built-in sleeper sofas, a dressing room, a bath, and a kitchenette. Its Victorian décor reflected the taste of Disney's wife, Lillian. A fire pole led downstairs for a quick exit; however, park employees had to block it off after one curious visitor climbed into the abode.

WALT DISNEY MAY NOT have made a home of his castle, but he did keep an apartment near one. During Disneyland's construction in 1954 and 1955, he insisted that the Main Street Fire Station be among the first buildings on the Anaheim lot—and with it,

WALT'S APARTMENT

a small apartment on the top floor. Disney spent many nights in his Main Street apartment, which allowed him to be omnipresent. He inspected everything— even in his bathrobe; each shrub, fence, pipe, building, stone, and coat of paint.

Disney planned a second apartment in New Orleans Square where he and his brother Roy could entertain dignitaries. The apartment would share a kitchen with the adjacent Club 33, a private restaurant for Disney's friends and business associates. However, Disney died shortly after the July 1967 opening of the Square, and the apartment now houses the Disney Gallery, which displays original concept sketches, architectural models, lithographs, and limited-edition pieces.

SEBASTIAN'S

Horatio Felonious Ignacious Crustaceous Sebastian's (Essence of) Stuffed Crab

INGREDIENTS:

1 sweet, succulent crab (like myself)
chilled, crisp lettuce leaves
1/2 oz dry bread crumbs
1 tbsp. olive oil
1/2 medium onion, finely chopped
1 clove garlic, chopped finely
2 oz tomatoes, finely chopped
2 tsp. finely chopped parsley
1/4 cup dry white wine
1/4 tsp. sugar
salt and pepper to taste
dash of cayenne
dab of flour

FOR SAUCE:

1. Heat oil in frying pan and sauté onion and garlic until soft.
2. Add tomatoes, and cook until the mixture is thick and well blended.
3. Add parsley, wine, sugar, salt, pepper, cayenne, and cook for 3–4 minutes over moderate heat.

FOR STUFFING:

Dress the insides of your crab shell with sauce (I have Chef Louis do this for me), add some flour—just a dab—roll shell around in some bread crumbs, and finally, squish a little leaf of lettuce wherever it may fit.

FOR ESSENCE:

1. Arrange remaining lettuce on silver platter.
2. Rest quietly on platter until served at the dinner table.
3. Scuttle away to safety at first opportunity.

SEAFOOD PLATTER

289

By 1960, MORE THAN 20 MILLION people had passed through the gates of Disneyland. Six new attractions had opened to rave reviews, and Disney was inspired to test the waters outside

1964 WORLD'S FAIR

California. The perfect opportunity arose with announcements of the World's Fair to be held in New York in 1964–65.

The fair would be a showcase for corporations, which Disney sought out for collaborative opportunities. Ford agreed to a Magic Skyway exhibit that would carry people through a dinosaur and Stone Age diorama. General Electric was also eager to work with Disney, especially with hopes of

improving its tarnished reputation after a price-fixing scandal: Disney proposed a rotating Audio-Animatronics household that would highlight the benefits of electricity. Pepsi Cola and UNICEF sponsored It's a Small World and the State of Illinois cast its support behind a lifelike orating model of President Lincoln.

All four exhibits were wildly popular. Sales rose for the represented companies, and in G.E.'s case in particular, public opinion polls proved distinctly favorable. At the fair's close, Disney moved the tried-and-true exhibits to Disneyland, and pushed forward with plans for a Florida theme park, confident that the Disney appeal could draw crowds on the east coast.

The G.E. Carousel of Progress ultimately moved to Walt Disney World in 1975; since 1964, the attraction has surpassed audience attendance for any other stage show seen in the history of American theater.

MOST WANTED

EMPEROR ZURG

CRIMES: attempted despotism, attempted planetary annihilation

KNOWN HANGOUT(S): infinity and beyond!

WARNING: ion blaster in wrist

DISTINGUISHING FEATURE(S): yellow teeth, glowing red eyes, purple everything else

112499

MADAME MEDUSA

062277

CRIMES: theft, kidnapping, holding teddy bear hostage

KNOWN HANGOUT(S): pawn shops, Devil's Bayou

ACCOMPLICE(S): Mr. Snoops (human), Nero and Brutus (crocodiles)

DISTINGUISHING FEATURE(S): wild red hair, red lips, big jewelry

CAPTAIN HOOK (ALIAS CODFISH)

CRIMES: attempted murder, piracy, kidnapping, terrorism

KNOWN HANGOUT(S): Skull Island, Mermaid Lagoon

ACCOMPLICE(S): Mr. Smee, Black Murphy, Mullins, Starkey, Skylights (pirates)

DISTINGUISHING FEATURE(S): powerful left hook

020553

062494

SCAR

CRIMES: fratricide, overthrow of governing body, inciting wildebeest riots

KNOWN HANGOUT(S): Pride Rock, Hyena Caverns

ACCOMPLICE(S): Shenzi, Banzai, and Ed (hyenas)

DISTINGUISHING FEATURE(S): scar (isn't that obvious?)

QUEEN, A.K.A.: WICKED STEPMOTHER, OLD HAG, WITCH

CRIMES: conspiracy, attempted murder, apple polishing, lousy parenting

KNOWN HANGOUT(S): castle balconies, dungeon, forest

ACCOMPLICE(S): Huntsman, Raven, Magic Mirror

DISTINGUISHING FEATURE(S): (in witch disguise) wart, single tooth, cackle

122137

111828

PETE, A.K.A.: BLACK PETE, PUTRID PETE, PEG-LEG PETE, BIG PETE, BIG BAD PETE, DIRTY PETE, BOOTLEG PETE, BOLD PETE, PIERRE DE FRAUD

CRIMES: assault, battery

KNOWN HANGOUT(S): steamboats, service stations, the House of Mouse

ACCOMPLICE(S): Maw Pete (mother), Sylvester Shyster, Weasel, Emil Eagle

DISTINGUISHING FEATURE(S): rarely seen sans cheap cigar

DISCOGRAPHY

FIREHOUSE FIVE PLUS TWO

DURING LUNCH HOURS in the 1940s, Disney animator Ward Kimball would gather his fellow coworkers and jazz enthusiasts around the phonograph and jam. With Kimball on trombone, Clarke Mallery on clarinet, Frank Thomas at the piano, Ed Penner on bass saxophone, and Jim MacDonald playing the drums, their sessions became so lively that when the phonograph broke down, they kept right on playing. The five players adopted the name Hugageedy 8 and later the San Gabriel Valley Blue Blowers.

By 1949, the band picked up two more regulars: Johnny Lucas on trumpet and Harper Goff on banjo. That spring, Kimball got the idea for the band to join a Horseless Carriage Club caravan from Los Angeles to San Diego. The only vehicle he could find big enough for the band that qualified for the caravan was a 1914 American LaFrance fire truck. So Kimball scored some vintage fire helmets and the group officially became the Firehouse Five Plus Two.

The Disney Studio crew of artists, writers, and directors started recording under the Good Time Jazz label and playing regularly at Hollywood nightclubs, benefits, and on radio programs. FH5+2 soared in popularity in the 1950s and 1960s with their brand of traditional jazz influenced by Jelly Roll Morton and Lu Watters plus humorous sound effects with brass fire bells, fire sirens, washboards, and vocals. Music critic George Avakian described FH5+2 in 1959 as "the happiest band I have heard in a long time."

Did you know? In one year, the Disneyland after-hours crew uses 1,000 brooms, 3,000 mops, 20,000 gallons of paint, and restocks 19,000 miles of toilet paper. Of the 12 million pounds of trash collected each year, the parks' recycling program reprocesses 2.4 million pounds of cardboard, 512,000 pounds of office paper, and 6,500 pounds of aluminum cans.

When the clock strikes midnight in Anaheim, California, Disneyland is closing its gates for the night. Meanwhile, across the Atlantic in Paris, it is 9 A.M., where crowds are gathering for the "rope drop" that signals the park's official opening. Regardless of the time of day, the day of the week, or the date on the calendar, someone is always working on the magic behind the scenes at the parks.

* Jungle Cruise hippos get their ears cleaned every night by certified divers.

* Web spinners "dust" the Haunted Mansion each night, strategically placing cobwebs and antique grime on hundreds of pieces of furniture.

* Brass buffers de-fingerprint all the brass in the parks to the tune of 1,200 quarts of brass polish per year.

* Engineers, technicians, and electricians conduct eagle-eye inspections of all the attractions' motors, tracks, electrical connections, fuses, sound systems, lighting, and moving parts.

* Gum removers use pressure cleaners, trowels, and chemical solvents to remove the sticky stuff from every surface, every day.

* Horticulturalists and gardeners trim hundreds of topiaries and tend thousands of trees, shrubs, and flowers.

* The dolls in It's a Small World— nearly 300 in all—get spruced up by the overnight crew.

* Dishwashers keep the gargantuan Mad Tea Party teacups clean and maintained.

* The moat surrounding Cinderella Castle gets early-morning scrubs before guests arrive in the park.

AT A TIME WHEN men dominated Disney's animation department, only Retta Scott, the studio's sole female animator, had advanced enough skills to tackle the wild dogs in *Bambi*. Supervising animator, Eric Larson, immediately recognized Scott's uncanny perception of canine anatomy, movement, and behavior, and assigned the scene to her.

"astounding ability to draw powerful, virile animals from almost any perspective and in any action."

Her work on the 1942 classic earned her a screen credit, making her the first female Disney artist to earn this distinction. Scott earned the respect of Disney's best

RETTA SCOTT: BEAUTIES AND BEASTS

animators, including Marc Davis, who claimed that "no one matched her ability" to draw animals from all angles. Scott's penchant for drawing creatures continued on *Dumbo* (1941) and the "Wind in the Willows" segment of *The Adventures of Ichabod and Mr. Toad* (1949), for which she created the weasels.

Scott joined the Disney Story department in 1938, and became the first woman to show interest in and ultimately join the animation department. Her portrayal of the frighteningly realistic hunting dogs proved to be among the most poignant scenes in *Bambi*. Animators Frank Thomas and Ollie Johnston revered Scott for her

In 1950, Scott left the studio for the East Coast and created artwork for Disney's licensee, Golden Books. In 2000, Disney Art Classics released a limited-edition color serigraph of Scott's cover artwork for the 1950 Big Golden Book, *Cinderella*. In 2001, Scott was honored posthumously with the Disney Legends Award.

id you know? Retta Scott's wild canines can be een in Richard Adams's animated sci-fi classic, *he Plague Dogs* (1982), directed by Martin Rosen.

WHEN THE BLUE FAIRY anointed Jiminy Cricket the official conscience of a wooden boy in *Pinocchio* (1940), that tall order may have been enough to ensure immortality. But unlike most characters introduced in animated features, the jocular cricket was a tough bug to keep down. Jiminy became Disney's educator, safety expert, and all-around host.

The lucky bug owed much of his success to the vocal performance of singer/actor Cliff Edwards, also known as Ukulele Ike. Edwards's classic performance as Jiminy singing "When You Wish Upon a Star" earned an Oscar for Best Song in

JIMINY CRICKET:

1940. Jiminy took center stage of the 1947 feature *Fun and Fancy Free* (in which the Cricket crooned "I'm a Happy-Go-Lucky Fellow," originally recorded for *Pinocchio*).

Jiminy found his greatest fame apart from Pinoke on television. In creating the *Mickey Mouse Club*, Walt Disney envisioned him as the shining star. "Our old friend Jiminy Cricket will also be part of the show," Walt Disney told ABC affiliates in September 1955. "Jiminy's going to help us with what we call our factual entertainment. He'll show the youngsters things about the living world, about health, hygiene, safety, and many other things that concern their well-being." Thereafter, Jiminy featured prominently in newly created animation more than Mickey himself. From *I'm No Fool* to the *Encyclopedia* series, the cricket-turned-conscience made an indelible impression on audiences everywhere.

CONSCIENTIOUS GUIDE

And, Jiminy's career is still flourishing as he continues to represent The Walt Disney Company in many arenas, including his role as Ambassador of Environmental Awareness.

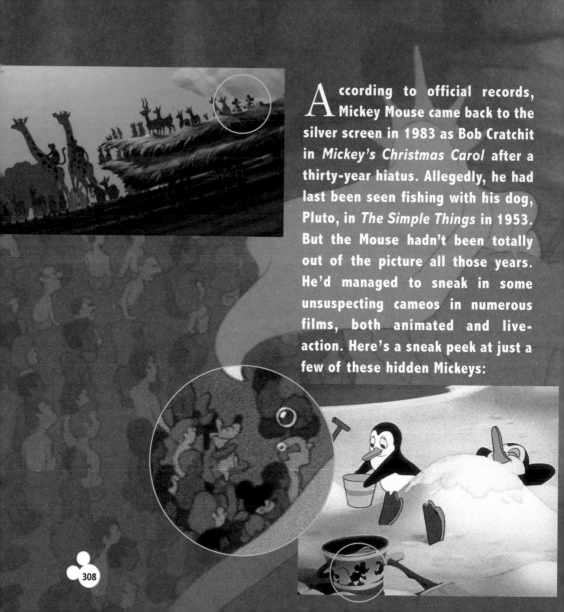

According to official records, Mickey Mouse came back to the silver screen in 1983 as Bob Cratchit in *Mickey's Christmas Carol* after a thirty-year hiatus. Allegedly, he had last been seen fishing with his dog, Pluto, in *The Simple Things* in 1953. But the Mouse hadn't been totally out of the picture all those years. He'd managed to sneak in some unsuspecting cameos in numerous films, both animated and live-action. Here's a sneak peek at just a few of these hidden Mickeys:

The Three Caballeros (1945). Mickey decorates a sand pail during a sequence with Pablo the Penguin.

The Rescuers (1977). Strategically hidden in a watch face, Mickey adorns the wall of the Rescue Aid Society's headquarters.

Who Framed Roger Rabbit (1988). Mickey shares an office with R. K. Maroon . . . as a figurine on the table.

Oliver & Company (1988). Mickey hangs around with cat-napper Fagan's timekeepers (on his wrist).

The Little Mermaid (1989). Invited by King Triton himself, Mickey and his friends share orchestra seating during the mermaid concert.

The Nightmare Before Christmas (1993). Mickey makes Christmas Eve cozy for children who receive a bat doll and a bullet-riddled duck—as a pair of flannel pj's.

Toy Story (1995). Not only does Mickey keep time for Andy in a big wristwatch clock, but he has special meaning for the Megadork rock star who sports a Mickey tattoo.

101 Dalmatians (1996). Mickey's always ready for mealtimes in Roger and Anita's home, where he hangs out on the shelf behind the kitchen table.

Jungle 2 Jungle (1997). Michael Cromwell receives a Mickey Mouse birthday card, which he displays on his desk in his office.

Fantasia/2000 (2000). Not one to be left behind, Mickey takes Minnie's hand and joins the parade of animals boarding Noah's Ark.

FOR DECADES couples had requested permission to tie the knot in the Magic Kingdom, and in 1991 Walt Disney World made it possible with the opening of their Fairy Tale Weddings Department. Since then, more than 15,000 lovebirds have exchanged vows at the resort, and newlyweds have made it the nation's most popular honeymoon destination.

HAPPILY EVER AFTER

Couples could choose to marry in front of Cinderella Castle, in World Showcase at Epcot, and in many of the Walt Disney World resorts. Then, in 1995, Walt Disney World opened its Victorian-style Wedding Pavilion. Designed to seat up to 250 people, the pavilion offers ideal views of Cinderella Castle. Brides and grooms can create *their* perfect day from a simple intimate ceremony to the ultimate elegant fairy tale fantasy. For the true Disney-lover, Cinderella's Coach and Mickey, Minnie, and other favorite characters can join the celebration during the reception.

BY M. HATTER AND M. HARE

1. Always have plenty of clean teacups and empty chairs. When your cup is empty, simply move to the next chair.

2. Remember to be invited, or else it's very rude (indeed!) to sit at the table.

3. Offer unbirthday cakes to anyone who compliments your singing. (And be sure to mind the explosives.)

4. If you haven't had any tea, you can't very well take less, but you can always take more.

5. When telling stories, always start at the beginning. When you get to the end, stop.

6. If you don't think, you shouldn't speak.

7. If you don't care for tea, at least make polite conversation.

8. Never, ever speak of cats when dormice are present.

9. If anything starts to make sense, simply change the subject. Try asking a riddle.

10. If you don't have time for a cup of tea, your watch is probably two days slow. The best way to fix it is with slabs of butter, two spoons, jam, and lemon. (But not mustard . . . that would be much too silly.)

THE BEST-KNOWN American star of the silver screen in 1930 wasn't Greta Garbo or Robert Montgomery, but an animated phenomenon, Mickey

THE ORIGINAL

Mouse. The first Mickey Mouse Club was the brainchild of Harry W. Woodin, Fox Dome Theater manager in Ocean Park, California. Woodin recognized that at a time when the United States economy was at an all-time low, Mickey Mouse helped generate box-office magic in movie theaters throughout the country.

In September 1929, Woodin approached Walt Disney with the idea of organizing a Mickey Mouse theater club for children. Saturday afternoon matinees that featured Mickey Mouse cartoons would establish a solid theater patronage for Woodin and open new windows of opportunity for Disney. The plan worked. At the stroke of noon, Saturday, January 11, 1930, the first Mickey Mouse Club gathered at the Fox Dome Theater. With promises of free membership cards, buttons, activities, contests, birthday celebrations, and prizes, Mickey Mouse Clubs quickly sprouted in

MICKEY MOUSE CLUB

hundreds of theaters, to the delight of children, as well as parents, teachers, and local merchants.

By 1932, the clubs had boomed; 800 movie theaters worldwide sponsored Mickey Mouse Clubs. Membership in the United States soared into the millions, rivaling the total memberships in the Boy Scouts and Girl Scouts of America combined.

MICKEY MOUSE CLUB

HERE IS THE OFFICIAL MICKEY MOUSE
CLUB MEMBERSHIP CARD

MEMBER **MICKEY MOUSE** CLUB

_____ Theatre

This Certifies that

is a Registered Member of the
MICKEY MOUSE CLUB

See Reverse Side

Chief Mickey Mouse

AND HERE IS THE OFFICIAL MICKEY
MOUSE BUTTON

Membership Card and Button, illustrated at left, will be given Boys and Girls FREE upon presentation of Membership Application Forms properly filled out. Application Blanks can be obtained FREE from OFFICIAL MICKEY MOUSE STORES listed on Back Page. Get Your Membership Card and Button, Boys and Girls —They're Going to be Valuable and Helpful in Many Ways. Surprises Prize Offers, Special Rewards and Many Other Attractive Events are Being Arranged for Members in Good Standing and a Member in Good Standing is a Boy or Girl who Secures and Carries a Membership Card and Wears the Mickey Mouse Club Button at all times.

MICKEY MOUSE CLUB CREED

I will be a square shooter in my home, in school, on the playgrounds, where-ever I may be.

I will be truthful and honorable and strive, always, to make myself a better and more useful little citizen.

I will respect my elders and help the aged, the helpless and children smaller than myself.

In short, I will be a good American!—

MICKEY MOUSE CLUB

KANSAS CITY IN 1923 meant tough times for 21-year-old Walt Disney. His endeavors with Laugh-O-gram Films left him in the red. Desperate to turn a profit, Walt filmed four-year-old Virginia Davis against a plain backdrop with the intent of combining the footage with a cartoon. The pilot, titled *Alice's Wonderland*, wasn't the first marriage of live action and animation, yet it differed in concept and was the first to have a female lead. Disney hoped to sell potential distributors on the idea of an entire series of Alice's adventures in cartoonland.

New York cartoon distributor Margaret J. Winkler responded favorably, encouraging Walt to forge ahead with production. But halfway through, Laugh-O-gram went bankrupt. Despondent, Walt left Kansas City with $40 and hopped a train for Hollywood to start over.

ALICE COMEDIES

Once in California, Walt convinced his creditors to ship *Alice's Wonderland* to Winkler for review. Her response: $1,500 per negative. Her stipulation: Virginia Davis needed to be in the films. Walt convinced

the Davis family to come to Hollywood; thus began the Alice Comedies.

Walt knew he could never be a top-notch animator, so he sent for another of his Kansas City colleagues and the best artist he knew, Ub Iwerks. With Iwerks's arrival in June 1924, Walt gave up his career as an animator and focused on his strengths: story and direction. By 1927, the Disney studio produced 56 Alice Comedies, which eventually featured three subsequent Alice stars.

When Charles Mintz married Winkler, he assumed her business and pushed to end the Alice series, which relied heavily on gags, not plot. Mintz wanted a rabbit. Walt jumped at the opportunity, and Alice gave way to Oswald the Lucky Rabbit.

Walt Disney's fascination with trains started in his childhood in the Midwest. He rode them every chance he got, and even credited one train ride as the inspiration for his greatest and most widely loved creation—the Mouse.

From the railway for the miniature train Lilly Belle that Walt built in his backyard (which included a tunnel under his wife, Lillian's, flower beds) to the futuristic railway of Tomorrowland, the World of Disney has celebrated the iron horse in many ways. Here is a sampling of the past and present Disney trains:

RETIRED

Santa Fe and Disneyland Railroad
Rainbow Caverns Mine Train
Mine Train through Nature's Wonderland
Fort Wilderness Railway

ACTIVE TODAY

Disneyland Railroad
    E. P. Ripley
    C. K. Holliday
    Fred G. Gurley
    Ernest S. Marsh
Casey Jr. Circus Train
Eureka
Le Petit Train du Cirque
Big Thunder Mountain Railroad
The Disneyland Monorail
Engine No. 5

ON THE SILVER SCREEN

The Great Locomotive Chase starring:
    B & O's William Mason as the "General"
    B & O's Inyo as the "Texas"

Did you know? The Monsanto House of the Future was so well built that when the demolition crew tried to dismantle it, the wrecking ball bounced off the exterior. Workers had to go in with crowbars and take it apart by hand.

SPACE STATION X-1

Look into the future...
See America from
OUTER SPACE

TOMORROWLAND

YESTERDAY'S TOMORROWLAND

Walt Disney envisioned Tomorrowland as an evolving glimpse into the future. But as tomorrow's innovations fade into today's standard fare, time comes for the old attractions to make way for the new. Tomorrowland's retirees:

- 1955–1958 Richfield Oil's The World Beneath Us
- 1955–1960 Kaiser Aluminum's Hall of Fame
- 1955–1960 Monsanto Hall of Chemistry
- 1955–1960 Space Station X-1, renamed Satellite View of America in 1958
- 1955–1966 20,000 Leagues Under the Sea (the original Tomorrowland entrance)
- 1955–1967 Monsanto House of the Future
- 1955–1966 Thimble Drome Flight Circle, a.k.a. Tomorrowland Rocket and Flight Circle
- 1956–1958 Phantom Boats
- 1956–1960 Crane Co.'s Bathroom of Tomorrow
- 1956–1994 Skyway to Tomorrowland/Skyway to Fantasyland
- 1961–1966 Flying Saucers
- 1967–1973 General Electric's Carousel of Progress
- 1967–1985 Monsanto Adventure Thru Inner Space
- 1967–1995 PeopleMover
- 1955–1966 Rocket to the Moon, renamed Flight to the Moon (1967–1975), then renamed Mission to Mars (1975–1992)
- 1974–1998 America Sings

The music of Disney films has been made memorable by a wide range of artists, from classical composers to modern pop stars. Here are a few of the music makers:

Howard Ashman • Johann Sebastian Bach • Ludwig van Beethoven • George Bruns • Sonny Burke • Sammy Cahn • Frank Churchill • Phil Collins • Eliot Daniel • Mack David • Walt Disney • Paul Dukas • Danny Elfman • Sir Edward Elgar • Sammy Fain • George Gershwin • Ray Gilbert • Terry Gilkyson • Leigh Harline • Al Hoffman • Sir Elton John • Peggy Lee • Mel Leven • James Levine • Jerry Livingston • Henry Mancini • Alan Menken • Larry Morey • Modest Musorgsky • Randy Newman • Edward H. Plumb • Amilcare Ponchielli • Sergi Prokofiev • Ottorino Respighi • Sir Tim Rice • Camille Saint-Saëns • Stephen Schwartz • Richard M. Sherman • Robert B. Sherman • Dmitri Shostakovich • Franz Schubert • Paul J. Smith • Stephen Sondheim • Sting • Leopold Stokowski • Igor Stravinsky • Piotr Ilyich Tchaikovsky • Oliver Wallace • Ned Washington • Andrew Lloyd Webber • Matthew Wilder • Allie Wrubel • Hans Zimmer • David Zippel

DISNEY LEGENDS

In 1987, the Walt Disney Company began inducting honorees into a special hall of fame known as the Disney Legends. Much like the famed Hollywood Stars, Disney Legends are honored in cement with a bronze emblem, signatures, and handprints. The Disney Legends so far include:

Lucien Adés • James Algar • Bob Allen • Rex Allen • Tim Allen • Ken Anderson • Julie Andrews • Angel Angelopoulos • X. Atencio • Grace Bailey • Buddy Baker • Carl Barks • Kathryn Beaumont • Antonio Bertini • Armand Bigle • Mary Blair • Wally Boag • Roger E. Broggie • Fulton Burley • Harriet Burns • Gaudenzio Capelli • Joyce Carlson • Adriana Caselotti • Les Clark • Claude Coats • Pinto Colvig • Mary Costa • Bill Cottrell • Don DaGradi • Marc Davis • Marvin Davis • Virginia Davis • Roberto de Leonardis • Roy E. Disney • Jimmie Dodd • Ron Dominguez • Buddy Ebsen • Cyril Edgar • Cliff Edwards • Peter Ellenshaw • Don Escen • Morgan ("Bill") Evans • Becky Fallberg • Wally Feignoux • Norm Ferguson • Didier Fouret • Joseph Fowler • Van France • Annette Funicello • William Garity • Mario Gentilini • Betty Lou Gerson • Blaine Gibson • Harper Goff • Yale Gracey • Joe Grant • David Hand • Jack Hannah • John Hench • Winston Hibler •

Sterling Holloway • Dick Irvine • Ub Iwerks • Wilfred ("Jaxon") Jackson • Cyril James • Glynis Johns • Ollie Johnston • Dean Jones • Dickie Jones • Bill Justice • Milt Kahl • Kay Kamen • Paul Kenworthy • Ward Kimball • Horst Koblischek • Al Konetzni • Larry Lansburgh • Angela Lansbury • Eric Larson • Jack Lindquist • John Lounsbery • Irving Ludwig • Ham Luske • Jim Macdonald • Sam McKim • Fred MacMurray • Gunnar Mansson • Bill Martin • Bob Matheison • Ed Meck • Hayley Mills • Alfred Milotte • Elma Milotte • Arnoldo Mondadori • Bob Moore • Fred Moore • Clarence ("Ducky") Nash • Dick Nunis • Ken O'Connor • Armand Palivoda • Norman ("Stormy") Palmer • Fess Parker • Poul Brahe Pedersen • Bill Peet • William E. ("Joe") Potter • Thurl Ravenscroft • Wolfgang ("Woolie") Reitherman • Lloyd L. Richardson • Charlie Ridgway • Dodie Roberts • Wathel Rogers • Kurt Russell • Herb Ryman • Retta Scott • Ben Sharpsteen • Richard M. Sherman • Robert B. Sherman • Paul Smith • Masatomo Takahashi • Donn B. Tatum • Betty Taylor • Frank Thomas • Ruthie Thompson • Vladimir ("Bill") Tytla • Dick Van Dyke • André Vanneste • E. Cardon ("Card") Walker • Bill Walsh • Roy Williams • Paul Winkler • Frank G. Wells • Matsuo Yokoyama

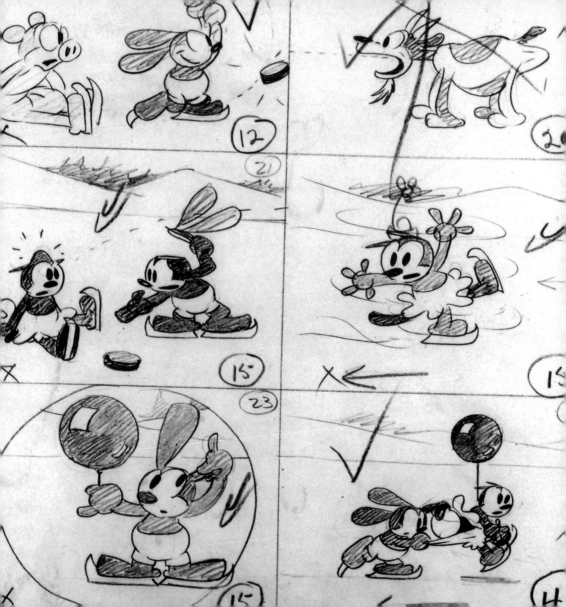

Before the days of "talkies," Walt Disney's first Hollywood foray into animated films starred a plucky rabbit named Oswald, who captured his audience through a series of clever gestures and amusing gags. Between 1927 and 1928, Universal distributed a new Oswald adventure in theaters as quickly as Disney's artists could animate them—every two weeks.

1   *Poor Papa*

2   *Trolley Troubles*

3   *Oh, Teacher*

4   *Great Guns*

5   *The Mechanical Cow*

6   *All Wet*

7   *The Ocean Hop*

8   *The Banker's Daughter*

9   *Harem Scarem*

10 *Rickety Gin*

11 *Neck 'n' Neck*

12 *Empty Socks*

13 *The Ol' Swimmin' 'Ole*

14 *Africa Before Dark*

15 *Rival Romeos*

16 *Bright Lights*

17 *Sagebrush Sadie*

18 *Ride 'em Plow Boy*

19 *Ozzie of the Mounted*

20 *Hungry Hoboes*

21 *Oh, What a Knight*

22 *Sky Scrappers*

23 *The Fox Chase*

24 *Tall Timber*

25 *Sleigh Bells*

26 *Hot Dog*

Did you know? Oswald the Lucky Rabbit became the first Disney character to appear on merchandise—an Oswald stencil set, a chocolate-covered marshmallow candy bar, and a pin-backed button.

ART CAPTIONS

p. 1. Detail of poster art from the Mickey Mouse short, *The Moose Hunt* (1931).

p. 2. Buddy Ebsen models for Walt Disney as the "Dancing Man." Ebsen's routine, complete with sound, provided live-action reference for the first Audio-Animatronics figure in 1949.

p. 5. Walt Disney shows off colors created by the Ink and Paint Girls on *The Wonderful World of Color*.

p. 10. Roy E. Disney shares a moment with Mickey in front of Cinderella Castle in Walt Disney World.

pp. 12–13. Walt Disney takes his daughter, Diane, and grandson, Christopher, for a spin through Tomorrowland's Autopia at Disneyland.

pp. 20–21. Eye to eye with Doc, the wisest of the seven dwarfs, as he can be seen at the Disney theme parks.

pp. 26–27. Slim, Gypsy, Rosie, and Dim from Disney/Pixar *A Bug's Life* (1998) in a forest of clover. Production still.

pp. 34–35. Production still from the "Pink Elephants on Parade" sequence in *Dumbo*, 1941. When Dumbo accidentally gets drunk on champagne-spiked water, he experiences psychedelic elephantine hallucinations.

pp. 42–43. Eyvind Earle gouache development art for *Sleeping Beauty*, (1959). As the supervising color stylist and sketch artist for *Sleeping Beauty*, Earle took his inspiration from Gothic tapestries, Persian miniatures, and the paintings of fifteenth- and sixteenth-century artists Albrecht Dürer, Jan van Eyck, and Pieter Bruegel.

pp. 50–51. *Fantasia/2000* Sprite whose tears revive the land during Igor Stravinski's "Firebird Suite" segment, the brainchild of directors Paul and Gaëtan Brizzi. The segment explores the theme of life, death, and renewal.

pp. 58–59. The Skyway to Fantasyland/ Skyway to Tomorrowland operated at Disneyland from 1956 to 1994. Four-passenger gondolas offered sightseers a fantastical glimpse of the Alps as they passed through the Matterhorn.

pp. 66–67. Pastel for *Bambi* by inspirational sketch artist Tyrus Wong. During his short tenure at the Disney Studio (1938–1941), Wong created hundreds of paintings, water-colors, and pastels that ultimately shaped the visual style and color for *Bambi* (1942).

pp. 74–75. The Monorail peeks out from behind a floral display in Walt Disney World.

pp. 78–79. Computer wireframe rendering of Sid Philips, Andy's neighbor and the toys' nemesis in *Toy Story* (1995).

pp. 82–83. Mickey Mouse and Donald Duck get ready to greet the first visitors of Disneyland on opening day, July 17, 1955.

pp. 88–89. Character designer and story artist Joe Grant and Walt Disney review storyboard art from Igor Stravinsky's "Rite of Spring" segment of *Fantasia* (1940).

pp. 92–93. In this production still from *So Dear to My Heart* (1949), Wise Old Owl delivers his lessons in song to Danny the lamb.

pp. 100–101. Background art of Notre Dame de Paris by Don Moore from *The Hunchback of Notre Dame* (1996).

pp. 108–109. Detail of a silkscreen print of a pirate adventure map created by Imagineer John Horny for Disneyland Paris. A replica of the print adorns the walls of the cruise ship *Disney Magic*.

pp. 112–113. Production still of Ursula, the voluptuous, villainous Sea Witch, who vies for Ariel's soul in *The Little Mermaid* (1989). Voiced by Emmy Award–winning actress Pat Carroll.

pp. 118–119. The Disney Store as it appeared in New York City's Times Square, adjacent to The New Amsterdam Theatre.

pp. 126–127. Snow White enjoys a dance with an extra-tall Dopey (who gets a boost from Sneezy in Walt Disney's first feature-length animated film, *Snow White and the Seven Dwarfs* (1937).

pp. 130–131. Concept art by Michael Giaimo for *Pocahontas* (1995).

pp. 134–135. Sample stock certificate from 1988 for The Walt Disney Company.

pp. 140–141. Detail of Horace Horsecollar model sheet. One of Mickey Mouse's oldest barnyard buddies, Horace first appeared in *The Plow Boy* (1929) as Mickey's trusted steed.

pp. 146–147. A bird's-eye view of the Dumbo Flying Elephants attraction at Disneyland. Pachyderm flight operators can soar high and low by moving individual levers.

pp. 154–155. Production still of Hercules battling the dreaded, three-headed Hydra in *Hercules* (1997). The Hydra owes much of its look to drawings by inspirational sketch artist Gerald Scarfe; also known for his distinctive style in the animation sequences of Pink Floyd's *The Wall* (1982).

pp. 162–163. Shaman Rafiki, along with proud parents King Mufasa and Queen Sarabi, presents the new heir to the throne, young Simba, before the entire congregation of Pridelands animals in the New York production of *The Lion King: Pride Rock on Broadway*.

pp. 168–169. Poster art created for the 1940 release of *Fantasia*; the rereleases in the '50s and '60s; and the release of *Fantasia/2000*.

pp. 172–173. Voiced by Bob Newhart and Eva Gabor, Bernard and Bianca team up in *The Rescuers* (1977) and *The Rescuers Down Under* (1990). Production still.

pp. 176–177. Mickey and Minnie greet guests at Tokyo Disneyland in their finest kimonos.

pp. 180–181. Disneyland admittance ticket, #1.

pp 186–187. Harlem jazz drummer Duke the Riveter livens the George Gershwin "Rhapsody in Blue" segment of *Fantasia/2000*. The life-affirming segment was developed by the husband-and-wife director–art director team of Eric and Susan Goldberg.

pp. 192–193. Disney Publishing Archive illustration from *Peter and the Wolf* segment of *Make Mine Music* (1955), narrated by Sterling Holloway.

pp. 194–195. Album covers of some of Disney's perennial best-selling sound tracks: *Song of the South*, featuring Academy Award-winning song "Zip-a-Dee-Doo-Dah" as sung by James Baskett; *The Jungle Book*, with the scat-jazz music of Louis Prima; "It's a Small World" offering international folk songs by the Disneyland Boys' Choir; Walt Disney's The Enchanted Tiki Room featuring "Let's All Sing Like the Birdies Sing"; and Holidays with the Mouseketeers with a song for every holiday.

pp. 202–203. New York City premiere of *Pocahontas*, June 10, 1995. Thousands of people gathered on Central Park's Great Lawn in front of four massive screens for a first look at the Academy Award–winning film.

pp. 210–211. In 1968, the United States issued a six-cent postage stamp featuring Walt Disney and children from "It's a Small World." Since then, Disney characters have adorned postcards and letters in a host of countries worldwide.

pp. 216–217. One of the original concept sketches by Mary Blair for the 1964 World's Fair exhibit, It's a Small World. Blair's sense of color and style dominate the design of the attraction, which was permanently relocated to Disneyland on May 28, 1966.

pp. 222–223. Production still of Aladar and Bruton from *Dinosaur* (2000).

pp. 232–233. Visual development artwork of Ariel in her secret grotto by Andy Gaskill for *The Little Mermaid* (1989).

pp. 238–239. Dinah and Pluto fall madly in love in *Pluto's Heart Throb* (1950).

pp. 246–247. Sample pages from a press book that details *Sleeping Beauty* (1959) merchandise available through Disney's licensees.

pp. 252–253. Mickey and friends perform in the "75 Years of Disney Magic" ice show commemorating the 75th anniversary of The Walt Disney Company. Since 1981, Feld Entertainment has produced Disney on Ice, which stages more than 1,800 performances in more than 44 countries per year, often in the language of the country in which it's performed.

pp. 258–259. Fireworks fill the night sky for the October 1, 1999, christening ceremony of the *Disney Wonder* in Port Canaveral, Florida. The *Wonder* joins the *Disney Magic* as the second cruise ship built for Disney Cruise Line.

pp. 266–267. Original lobby cards, the display placards that appear in movie theater lobbies, depict starring characters in *20,000 Leagues Under the Sea* (1971), *Robin Hood* (1976), and *The Incredible Journey* (1963).

pp. 274–276. Visual development for *Beauty and the Beast* (1991) by West German-born painter and designer Hans Bacher. As production designer, his stylized artwork also influenced the look of *Mulan* (1998).

pp. 282–283. Love, Las Vegas Style. In the summer of '69, a Las Vegas, Nevada, drive-in movie theater participated in a special Love Bug festival for the #1 movie of the year. More than one thousand VW Beetles (and their owners) gathered for an outdoor screening of *The Love Bug*.

p. 290–291. Story sketch and poster (inset) from the 1932 Silly Symphony *Flowers and Trees*. Shot in Technicolor, the film marks the release of the first color cartoon. *Flowers and Trees* is also the first film for which Walt Disney won an Academy Award, for Best Cartoon Short Subject.

pp. 296–297. Detail of poster for *Mickey's Revue* (1932), the forty-first Mickey Mouse cartoon. Starring the Mouse "in his latest rollicking laff riot," this film marks the debut of a nameless character who would become one of Mickey's best buddies, Goofy.

pp. 304–305. Concept art for *Winnie the Pooh and the Honey Tree* (1966).

pp. 312–313. A kiss is but a kiss, Disney-style. Clockwise from upper left: Lumiere and Cogsworth from *Beauty and the Beast* (1991); Cleo and Figaro from *Pinocchio* (1940); Prince Phillip and Princess Aurora from *Sleeping Beauty* (1959); Preston Whitmore and Thaddeus Thatch from *Atlantis* (2001); Donald and Daisy from *Fantasia/2000* (2000).

pp. 318–319. Aliens in the Pizza Planet "Claw Tank" from Sid's point of view in *Toy Story* (1995).

pp. 324–325. The Lionel Mickey Mouse Hand Car sold for $1 in 1934. The hand-painted metal windup cars were the hottest sellers that Christmas. Demand outstripped supply; the Lionel Corporation produced 253,000 red, green, orange, and maroon handcars—97,000 short of total store orders for 1934.

pp. 330–331. Accompanied by Hyacinth Hippo from *Fantasia* and the Dwarfs from *Snow White and the Seven Dwarfs*, band-leader Mickey Mouse gets ready to beat the big base drum led by Pluto and Goofy in this October 1964 "Character Parade" at Disneyland.

CONTRIBUTORS

As with any Disney project, everything is in the details, and this Little Big Book could not have been possible without the contribution, assistance, and dedication of an entire team of crackerjack people. First and foremost, a very special thank you to Roy E. Disney for his enthusiasm about this project. At Disney Editions thanks goes to Wendy Lefkon for her supreme guidance and wisdom; to Sara Baysinger for her passion and editorial leadership; to Jody Revenson for her plethora of research and brainstorms; to Monica Mayper for her patience and sticktoitivity; and to Christopher Caines for his keen editorial eye and brilliant sense of humor. At Welcome Enterprises, thanks goes to the unsinkable Alice Wong at the helm of production and Jon Glick for his perseverance and artistic craft. Exceptional thanks to Ed Squair at the Walt Disney Photo Library and Jim Fanning at Creative Services for their commitment to hunting down hundreds of pictures and hard-to-find gems; to Robert Tieman and Dave Smith at the Walt Disney Archives for their invaluable research and knowledge. Most especially, thanks to Mary Lippold at Studio Legal, Kevin Breen at Feature Animation, and Muriel Caplan at Disney Publishing for poring through scores of pages, fact-checking, and keeping our ducks in order.

For their contributions in creativity, ideas, research, and writing, additional accolades go to:

Kevin Banks
(Walt Disney World Resort Synergy)

Anita Bonnell
(CalArts Public Relations Office)

Darren Chiapetta
(Walt Disney World Resort Synergy)

Hugh Chitwood
(Walt Disney Imagineering)

Andrea Finger
(The Celebration Company)

David Fisher
(Walt Disney Imagineering)

Tom Fitzgerald
(Walt Disney Imagineering)

Bruce Gordon
(Walt Disney Imagineering)

Scott Groller
(CalArts Public Relations Office)

Don Hahn
(Walt Disney Feature Animation)

Ann Hansen
(Animation Research Library)

Michael Horn
(Corporate Legal)

Donna Kerley
(Disney Publishing Archives)

Kari Miller
(The Walt Disney Studios Creative Services)

Greg Montz
(Disney Cruise Line)

Peter Nolan
(Corporate Legal)

Yvonne O'Neill
(Walt Disney World Resort Special Events)

Kevin Rafferty
(Walt Disney Imagineering)

Victoria Saxon
(Disney Publishing & Creative Development)

Thomas Schumacher
(Walt Disney Feature Animation)

Ken Shue
(Disney Publishing & Creative Development)

Laura Simpson
(Walt Disney World Resort Synergy)

Marty Sklar
(Walt Disney Imagineering)

Lella Smith
(Animation Research Library)

Cindy Tamasi
(Disney Publishing Worldwide)

Rich Thomas
(Disney Publishing Worldwide)

Fred Tio
(The Walt Disney Studios Creative Services)

James Utt
(Walt Disney World Resort Special Events)

Finally, special thanks to: Kellie Nixon
at Peppino's Ristorante Italiano in Killington,
Vermont; the librarians at Brooklyn
Public Library; and the videophiles
at Cinematèque in Park Slope.

BIBLIOGRAPHY

BOOKS

Birnbaum's Disneyland 2001.
New York: Disney Editions, 2000.

*Birnbaum's Walt Disney World
2001.* New York: Disney
Editions, 2000.

*Birnbaum's WDW for Kids by
Kids 2001.* New York: Disney
Editions, 2000.

*Birnbaum's WDW Without Kids,
2001.* New York: Disney
Editions, 2000.

Brandon, Pam. *Walt Disney
World Resort: A Magical Year
by Year Journey, 1998.*
New York: Hyperion, 1998.

Bright, Randy. *Disneyland Inside
Story.* New York: Harry N.
Abrams, Inc., 1987.

Canemaker, John. *Before the
Animation Begins: The Art
and Lives of Disney Inspirational
Sketch Artists.* New York:
Hyperion, 1996.

Clute, John, and John Grant.
The Encyclopedia of Fantasy.
London: Orbit, 1999.

Cook, David A. *A History of
Narrative Film.* New York:
W.W. Norton & Co., 1981.

Cook, Deanna F., and the Experts
at *FamilyFun* Magazine. *Disney's
Family Cookbook: Irrististible
Recipes for You and Your Kids.*
New York: Hyperion, 1996.

Cotter, Bill. *The Wonderful
World of Disney Television:
A Complete History.* New York:
Hyperion, 1997.

Cunningham, Marion. *The Fanny
Farmer Cookbook.* New York:
Alfred A. Knopf, 1993.

Disney Cruise Line Travel Log.
New York: Hyperion, 1998.

*Disneyana: A Magical Year of
Classic Disney Collectibles 2001
Calendar.* Kansas City: Andrews
McMeel Publishing, 2000.

Dunlop, Beth. *Building a Dream:
The Art of Disney Architecture.*
New York: Harry N. Abrams, Inc.,
1996.

*Field Guide to Disney's Animal
Kingdom Theme Park.* New York:
Disney Editions, 2000.

Finch, Christopher. *The Art of
Walt Disney: From Mickey
Mouse to the Magic Kingdoms.*
New York: Harry N. Abrams, Inc.,
1975.

Finch, Christopher. *Disney's
Winnie the Pooh: A Celebration
of the Silly Old Bear.* New York:
Disney Editions, 2000.

*From the Fox & the Hound to
The Hunchback of Notre Dame.*
New York: Disney Press, 1996.

Funicello, Annette, and Patricia
Romanowski. *A Dream Is a Wish
Your Heart Makes.* New York:
Hyperion, 1994.

*Gardens of the Walt Disney
World Resort.* The Walt Disney
Company, 1992.

Gordon, Bruce, ed. *A Brush with
Disney: An Artist's Journey Told
Through the Words and Works of
Herbert Dickens Ryman.* Santa
Clarita, California: Camphor Tree
Publishers, 2000.

Grant, John. *Encyclopedia of Walt Disney's Animated Characters: From Mickey Mouse to Hercules.* New York: Hyperion, 1998.

Green, Amy Boothe, and Howard E. Green. *Remembering Walt: Favorite Memories of Walt Disney.* New York: Disney Editions, 1999.

Grunwald, Lisa, and Stephen J. Adler, eds. *America 1900-1999: Letters of the Century.* New York: Dial Press, 1999.

Hahn, Don. *Disney's Animation Magic.* New York: Disney Press, 2000.

Heide, Robert and John Gilman. *Disnayana: Classic Collectibles 1928–1958.* New York: Hyperion, 1994.

Heide, Robert and John Gilman. *The Mickey Mouse Watch: From the Beginning of Time.* New York: Hyperion, 1997.

Heminway, John. *Disney Magic: The Launching of a Dream.* New York: Hyperion, 1998.

Henderson, Mary. *The New Amsterdam: The Biography of a Broadway Theatre.* New York: Hyperion, 1997.

Henry, Bill, and Patricia Henry Yeomans. *An Approved History of the Olympic Games.* Alfred Publishing Co. Inc., 1984.

The Illustrated Treasury of Disney Songs. Milwaukee: Hal Leonard Corporation, and New York: Hyperion, 1998.

The Imagineers. *Walt Disney Imagineering: A Behind the Dreams Look at Making the Magic Real.* New York: Hyperion, 1996.

Iwerks, Leslie, and John Kenworthy. *The Hand Behind the Mouse.* New York: Disney Editions, 2001.

Johnson, Ollie, and Frank Thomas. *The Disney Villain.* New York: Hyperion, 1993.

Kieran, John, and Arthur Daley. *The Story of the Olympic Games 776 B.C. to 1964.* Philadelphia & New York: J. B. Lippincot Co., 1965.

Koenig, David. *Mouse Tales: A Behind-the-Ears Look at Disneyland.* Irvine, California: Bonaventure Press, 1994.

Krause, Martin, and Linda Witkowski. *Walt Disney's Snow White and the Seven Dwarfs: An Art in Its Making.* New York: Hyperion, 1994.

Kurtti, Jeff. *The Journal of Milo Thatch.* New York: Disney Editions, 2001.

Lambert, Pierre. *Mickey Mouse.* New York: Hyperion, 1998.

Maltin, Leonard. *The Disney Films, Fourth Edition.* New York: Disney Editions, 2000.

Neary, Kevin, and Dave Smith. *The Ultimate Disney Trivia Book.* New York: Hyperion, 1992.

Neary, Kevin, and Dave Smith. *The Ultimate Disney Trivia Book 3.* New York: Hyperion, 1997.

Neary, Kevin, and Dave Smith. *The Ultimate Disney Trivia Book 4.* New York: Disney Editions, 2000.

O'Day, Tim. *Disneyland: Celebrating 45 Years of Magic.* New York: Disney Editions, 2000.

One Day at Disney. New York: Hyperion, 1999.

Rawls, Walton. *Disney Dons Dogtags: The Best of Disney Military Insignia From World War II.* New York: Abbeville, 1992.

Ross, Andrew. *The Celebration Chronicles: Life, Liberty, and The Pursuit of Property Value in Disney's New Town.* New York: Ballantine Books, 1999.

Santoli, Lorraine. *Disney's California Adventure.* New York: Disney Editions, 2001.

Santoli, Lorraine. *The Official Mickey Mouse Club Book.* New York: Hyperion, 1995.

Shale, Richard. *Donald Duck Joins Up: The Walt Disney Studio During WWII.* Ann Arbor, Michigan: UMI Research Press, 1982.

Smith, Dave, and Steven Clark. *Disney: The First 100 Years.* New York: Hyperion, 1999.

Smith, Dave. *Disney A to Z: The Updated Official Encyclopedia.* New York: Hyperion, 1998.

Solomon, Charles. *The Disney That Never Was.* New York: Hyperion, 1995.

Thomas, Bob. *Building a Company: Roy O. Disney and the Creation of an Entertainment Empire.* New York: Hyperion, 1998.

Thomas, Bob. *Disney's Art of Animation: From Mickey Mouse to Hercules.* New York: Hyperion, 1997.

Thomas, Bob. *Walt Disney: An American Original.* New York: Hyperion, 1994.

Thomas, Frank, and Ollie Johnson. *The Illusion of Life: Disney Animation.* New York: Hyperion, 1981.

Walt Disney: Donald Duck. New York: Abbeville Press, 1978.

MISCELLANEOUS

The Walt Disney World Explorer CD-ROM. Burbank: Disney Interactive, 1996.

PERIODICALS

Close, Glenn. "Trust Me, It's Not Easy Being Cruella DeVil." *New York Times*, November 5, 2000.

Culhane, John. *"Fantasia/2000*: The Next Generation." *Disney Magazine,* Winter 1999-2000.

"The Evolution of the Space Shuttle." http://aerospacescholars.org

Ghez, Didier. Interview with Glen Keane, Walt Disney Feature Animation France, Montreuil: May 2, 1997. www.pizarro.net/didier/_private/interviu/Keane.html

Goldman, Albert. "Delirium of Disco." *Life,* November 1978.

Green, Amy Boothe. "Not Your Average Joe." *Disney Magazine,* Winter 1999-2000.

Green, Amy Boothe. "Rhetta Scott." The Disney Legends Awards ceremony program, October 12, 2000.

Green, Amy Boothe. "Words & Music By...." *Disney Magazine,* Summer 2000.

Hahn, Don. "Magical History Tour." *Disney Magazine,* Winter 1998-1999.

Heide, Robert, and John Gilman. "Depression Remedy." *Collectors' Showcase,* September/October 1999.

Heide, Robert, and John Gilman. "World War II Home Front." *Collectors' Showcase,* May/June 1999.

Laqua, Charsten. "Carl Barks: The Author." http://members.nbci.com/moneybin/author.html

Lyons, Mike. "The Mouse that Clark Built." www.kaleden.com/articles/1107.html

Markey, Kevin. "Imagine That!" *Disney Magazine,* Fall 1999.

McBride, Joseph. "Supercalifragilisticexpialidocious." *Daily Variety,* October 25, 1977.

McGilligan, Patrick. "Who is the World's Most Successful Director?" *American Film Magazine,* March 1978.

"Mickey's Children." *Life,* November 1978.

Oppenheimer, Lisa. "Disneyland After Dark." *Disney Magazine,* Summer 1999.

Pace, Eric. "Helen A. Mayer, Dumbo's Creator, Dies at 91." *The New York Times,* May 18, 1999.

Ross, Pippin. "The Ink & Paint Girls." *Disney Magazine,* Winter 1998-1999.

Santoli, Lorraine. "A Talent for Topiary." *Disney Magazine,* Summer 2000.

Smith, Hal. "For Whom the Brass Bell Tolls." Frisco Cricket, No. 8, Spring 1999.

"Von Braun: The Beginning of the Space Age." http://liftoff.msfc.nasa.gov

"Who's Who in Duckburg: The Number One Dime." http://victorian.fortunecity.com/palace/439/characters/dime.html

Wiley, Kim Wright. "A Big Draw." *Disney Magazine,* Summer 2000.

Wiley, Kim Wright. "A Taste of Walt Disney World." *Disney Magazine,* Fall 2000.

Woolley, Lynn. "Good-bye Old Number One." www.belogical.com

Wright, Mike. "The Disney–Von Braun Collaboration and Its Influence on Space Exploration." Included in "Selected Papers from the 1993 Southern Humanities Conference." Huntsville, Alabama: Southern Humanities Press, 1993.

WEB SITES

Bob Clampett's Home Page. www.bobclampett.com

CalArts Office of Public Affairs. www.calarts.edu

DCML: Disney comics. http://stp.ling.uu.se/~starback/dcml

Disney. www.Disney.com

Disney's Hoo Zoo. www.jps.net/xephyr/rich/dzone/hoozoo/hoozoo.html

The Encyclopedia of Disney Animated Shorts. www.geocities.com/~eutychus55

Hidden Mickeys of Disney. www.hiddenmickeys.org

The Internet Movie Database. www.imdb.com

Welcome to Celebration, Florida. www.CelebrationFL.com

INDEX

ANSWERS:
p. 48: 1d, 2a, 3i, 4f, 5b, 6h, 7c, 8e, 9g, 10j
p. 94: ACROSS: 1. Sticktoitivity (*So Dear to My
Heart*) 4. Lilongo (*Three Caballeros*)
6. OoDeLally (*Robin Hood*) 7. ByeYumPumPum
(*The Happiest Millionaire*) 8. TwasBrillig (*Alice
in Wonderland*) 9. HigitusFigitus (*The Sword in
the Stone*) **DOWN:** 2. TicoTico (*Saludos Amigos*)
3. BluddleUddleUmDum (*Snow White and the
Seven Dwarfs*) 5. LaLaLu (*Lady and the Tramp*)